Bible Story Color, Draw, 'n' Learn

Grades 2-3

by

Ginny Swinson

Carson-Dellosa Publishing, LLC
Greensboro, North Carolina

Credits:
Extension Activities: Ginny Swinson and Michelle Medlock Adams
Cover Design and Illustration: Nick Greenwood
Layout Design: Nick Greenwood
Inside Illustrations: J. J. Rudisill

This book contains stories about Bible events. To maintain readability level for the intended audience, the author has paraphrased all stories and quotations within stories. In addition, age-appropriateness was considered when selecting the portions of stories to include. While every effort has been made to achieve a high level of accuracy, the stories in this book are not intended to replace the stories in the Bible. Teachers and parents are encouraged to consult their preferred version of the Bible to clarify stories or portions of stories as needed.

Printed in the USA ▪ All rights reserved.

ISBN 978-1-60418-756-4
04-193161151

Table of Contents

Table of Contents

Table of Contents

Answer Key

There is a missing element on each coloring page. Here are suggested missing elements, listed by coloring page number:

Page 7 birds and water animals	**Page 67** water in stream	**Page 127** mountains and people
Page 9 land animals	**Page 69** jar with torch inside	**Page 129** stormy sky and high waves
Page 11 snake	**Page 71** lion	**Page 131** fish, loaves of bread
Page 13 fruit	**Page 73** columns of the temple	**Page 133** Jesus walking on water
Page 15 animal mates	**Page 75** "Moab" and "Israel" on signs	**Page 135** coin
Page 17 rainbow	**Page 77** moon and stars	**Page 137** more sheep
Page 19 words in speech balloons	**Page 79** oil dripping from horn	**Page 139** liquid pouring on man's injuries
Page 21 supplies on animals' backs	**Page 81** slingshot and stone	**Page 141** broom or other cleaning items
Page 23 stars	**Page 83** flour and oil containers	**Page 143** mud in Jesus' hand
Page 25 tents	**Page 85** fire	**Page 145** wolf
Page 27 stairway to heaven	**Page 87** water of Jordan River	**Page 147** more pigs
Page 29 animals sent by Jacob	**Page 89** Esther's crown	**Page 149** Zacchaeus
Page 31 designs and colors on coat	**Page 91** statue	**Page 151** water pouring from pitcher
Page 33 sacks of grain	**Page 93** angel	**Page 153** fruit on healthy branch
Page 35 basket	**Page 95** more lions	**Page 155** coats and branches
Page 37 Baby Moses	**Page 97** stormy sky and high waves	**Page 157** bread and wine
Page 39 flames on bush	**Page 99** big fish	**Page 159** crown of thorns
Page 41 king's headdress and throne	**Page 101** Gabriel	**Page 161** pile of cloths
Page 43 more frogs	**Page 103** Baby Jesus	**Page 163** marks on hands
Page 45 marks on house	**Page 105** star of Bethlehem	**Page 165** fish and bread
Page 47 column of cloud	**Page 107** Mary and Joseph's belongings	**Page 167** rooster
Page 49 walls of water with path in middle	**Page 109** Jesus	**Page 169** tongues of fire
Page 51 more manna	**Page 111** hairy texture of tunic	**Page 171** beam of light
Page 53 water pouring from the rock	**Page 113** dove	**Page 173** broken chains
Page 55 stone tablets	**Page 115** bread in thought balloon	**Page 175** throne of God
Page 57 angel on end of box	**Page 117** fish	
Page 59 fruit hanging from pole	**Page 119** wine pouring into cup	
Page 61 red rope on window	**Page 121** man lying on mat	
Page 63 trumpets	**Page 123** seeds in each area	
Page 65 rain and clouds	**Page 125** woman's hand touching robe	

More Than Just a Coloring Book

From Adam and Eve to John's glimpse into heaven, this 176-page coloring book highlights major Bible stories such as Noah's ark and the birth of Jesus, as well as lesser-known stories including Elijah's chariot of fire and Gideon's small but mighty army.

In addition to fun coloring pages, *Bible Story Color, Draw, 'n' Learn* proclaims God's Word and offers simple prayers and thought-provoking questions guaranteed to inform and inspire young readers.

All stories and quotations within stories are paraphrased into child-friendly language. Although chapter and verse spans are cited, story portions were selected according to their age-appropriateness for the targeted audience.

Bonus Feature

As an added bonus, there is something or someone missing from each coloring page! Clues in the accompanying Bible story will help children decide what to add to the picture. Some children may need additional prompts and will have more success in pairs or group discussion. A word or phrase describing the missing element(s) appears upside down on the bottom of each coloring page. Teachers may want to cover the answer with correction fluid before making photocopies. An answer key (page 5) lists suggested missing elements.

Extension Activities

This unique coloring book also offers three extension activities at the bottom of each story that will encourage interaction between you and the children you love.

- **Say It!** features a Bible verse that relates to the page's Bible story. The Say It! extension activities are directly quoted from the Holy Bible, New International Version (NIV).
- **Pray It!** offers a simple, one-line prayer written in child-friendly language.
- **Explore It!** presents one reading comprehension question and one life application question that reflects a theme in the story.

Note: The NIV translation of the Lord's Prayer appears on page 128. Teachers and parents who would rather teach another version may cover this with a substitute before making photocopies. For additional information about the text of the stories, see page 2.

God Creates a Beautiful World

What's missing?

Missing: birds and water animals

God Creates a Beautiful World

Genesis 1:1–23

In the beginning, there were no plants, no animals, and no creatures of any kind. There was no land, no water, no sun, and no moon. There were no stars in the sky. There was only darkness and silence. Then, God created the heavens and the earth.

God said, "Let there be light." A great light filled the sky, and God saw that the light was good. That was the end of the first day.

God spent the next three days creating the earth. He made the land, the oceans and rivers, and the trees and flowers. He made the sun, the moon, and the twinkling stars. God looked at everything that He had created, and He saw that it was good. But, God wasn't finished yet.

On the fifth day, God created the animals that live in the water and in the air. He made birds to fill the sky. He made fish and other animals to live in the water. When God looked at everything that He had created, He was very pleased.

Say It! "In the beginning God created the heavens and the earth." Genesis 1:1

Pray It! Thank You, God, for making such a beautiful world for us to enjoy.

Explore It! Name two kinds of animals that God made on the fifth day. Why do you think that God made the world?

God Creates a Man and a Woman

What's missing?

Missing: land animals

God Creates a Man and a Woman

Genesis 1:24–31, 2:1–23, 3:20

On the sixth day, God made the animals that live on the land. God's work was not finished. He wanted someone to take care of the world that He had created. God decided to make a man in His likeness. He said, "I will make someone to watch over all of the fish, the birds, and the other living creatures on the earth."

God gathered dust from the earth and formed it into a man. God breathed life into the man and called him Adam. Then, God planted a wonderful garden for Adam. He called this beautiful place the Garden of Eden.

God did not want Adam to be alone in this garden, so He created a woman. Adam named her Eve. God looked at all that He had created. He saw the land and water, the plants and animals, and Adam and Eve. He was very happy with His creation. God was finished. On the seventh day, He rested.

Say It! "So God created man in his own image, in the image of God he created him; male and female he created them." Genesis 1:27

Pray It! Thank You, God, for making us Your very special creations.

Explore It! Why did God create a woman? How can you thank God for creating you?

A Snake in the Garden of Eden

What's missing?

Missing: snake

A Snake in the Garden of Eden

Genesis 2:16–17, 3:1–5

The Garden of Eden was filled with love, goodness, and joy. Plants sprouted, trees grew tall, and flowers bloomed. There was no sickness, no fighting, and no sadness.

God wanted Adam and Eve to enjoy the wonderful garden forever. God gave Adam an important rule. If he followed this rule, his life would always be happy and filled with wonderful things.

God told Adam that he could eat the fruit from any tree in the garden except one. God said, "If you eat the fruit from the tree of knowledge, you will die." Adam shared this rule with Eve.

One day, a snake crept into God's garden. The snake asked Eve, "Did God tell you not to eat the fruit from any of these trees?"

Eve replied, "There is only one tree that we should not eat from. If we eat the fruit from the tree of knowledge, God said that we will die."

The snake told Eve a lie. "You will not die," the snake said. "God does not want you to eat that fruit because it will make you as smart as God."

Eve wondered, "Should I listen to the snake, or should I believe God?" She had a very difficult decision to make.

Say It! "And the Lord God commanded the man, 'You are free to eat from any tree in the garden; but you must not eat from the tree of the knowledge of good and evil.'"
Genesis 2:16–17

Pray It! Help me, God, to be strong enough to always do what is right.

Explore It! What were Adam and Eve told not to eat? What rules are hard for you to obey?

Adam and Eve Leave the Garden

What's missing?

Missing: fruit

Adam and Eve Leave the Garden

Genesis 3:6–23

Eve looked at the fruit from the tree of knowledge. It looked ripe and juicy. She decided to listen to the sneaky snake instead of to God. She picked the fruit from the tree of knowledge and bit into it. It tasted delicious. Eve shared the fruit with Adam. Adam and Eve knew that they broke God's rule, and they felt very sad.

Later that day, God came into the Garden of Eden. Adam and Eve were afraid of God, so they hid behind some trees. God asked, "Where are you?"

Adam told God that he was hiding because he was afraid. God asked Adam if they ate the fruit from the tree of knowledge. Adam sadly said, "Yes. Eve told me to taste the fruit."

Eve told God, "The snake tricked me into eating the fruit. Then, I gave it to Adam."

God was not happy. He told the snake, "You will crawl on your belly and eat dust all the days of your life." Then, God told Adam and Eve to leave the beautiful garden that He had made especially for them. He said, "You chose to disobey Me. Now, you will not live forever. You will have to work hard every day for as long as you live."

It was a sad day in the Garden of Eden. Still, God loved Adam and Eve very much.

Say It! "Then the man and his wife heard the sound of the Lord God as he was walking in the garden in the cool of the day, and they hid from the Lord God among the trees of the garden." Genesis 3:8

Pray It! Thank You, God, for loving me even when I make mistakes.

Explore It! What happened to Adam and Eve after they disobeyed God? What happens when you do not obey your parents?

Noah Builds an Ark

What should there be more of in this picture?

Missing: animal mates

Noah Builds an Ark

Genesis 6–7

God saw that the people He created had become greedy and evil. He felt sad that their hearts had grown selfish.

God decided to create a great flood to destroy all life under the heavens. He said, "I will wipe everything from the earth. There will be no people. There will be no animals that walk or birds that fly."

But, God was happy with one man named Noah. Noah was a good man who always obeyed God. Noah and his wife had three sons. His sons were married too. God made a promise to save Noah and his family from the flood.

God told Noah to build a large boat called an ark. The ark would hold all of Noah's family and at least two of every living creature on the earth.

Noah began building the ark and gathering food just as God instructed. Mother and father animals that walked on the earth and flew in the sky came to Noah. He made room for all of them on the ark.

When the boat was finished, Noah led his family and the animals inside. Then, God shut the ark's door. The heavens opened. Rain fell for 40 days and 40 nights. Everything on the earth died. Noah, his family, and the animals on the ark stayed safe and dry.

Say It!   "Noah did everything just as God commanded him." Genesis 6:22

Pray It!   Dear God, help me to obey You.

Explore It!   Why was God angry at all of the people except Noah? Describe a time when you felt safe and dry during a storm.

God Sends a Rainbow

What's missing?

Missing: rainbow

God Sends a Rainbow

Genesis 7:19–24, 8–9

God created a great flood. The rain poured over the earth. All of the trees and mountains were underwater. Noah, his family, and all of the animals lived safely inside the ark. After 150 days, God sent a great wind to push away the water. The ark landed on top of a mountain.

Noah sent a raven to find land, but the bird flew in circles. Later, Noah sent a dove. The dove could not find a dry place to put its feet. Noah waited seven days and sent the dove again. This time, the dove returned with a fresh olive leaf in its beak. Noah knew that the water had gone down.

God told Noah, "It is time to leave the ark." Noah let his family out of the ark and freed the animals. Then, God promised Noah, "No matter how bad people act, I will not flood the earth again."

God created a beautiful rainbow in the sky to remind people of His promise. God told Noah, "Every time a rainbow appears in the clouds, I will remember My promise. My promise will last forever."

Say It! "'Whenever the rainbow appears in the clouds, I will see it and remember the everlasting covenant between God and all living creatures of every kind on the earth.'" Genesis 9:16

Pray It! God, we thank You for rainbows.

Explore It! Which bird brought back the olive leaf? What do you think of when you see a rainbow?

The Tower of Babel

What's missing?

Missing: mixed-up words in speech balloons

The Tower of Babel

Genesis 11:1–9

Many years after the great flood, people filled the earth again. Everyone in the world spoke the same language. Everyone could understand each other.

The people came together at a nice place near a river. They decided to settle there.

They said, "We can build a city here. We will make bricks out of mud and straw. We will build a tower that will reach to the heavens. Everyone will see how important we are."

God did not like this plan. He did not want people to act like God. He knew that they would get into trouble.

So, God made the people speak different languages. When the people tried to talk to each other, they could no longer understand each other's words.

The people stopped building the city and the tower. Then, God scattered the people to places all over the earth. The city was called Babel because Babel means a confusing language.

Say It! "That is why it was called Babel—because there the Lord confused the language of the whole world. From there the Lord scattered them over the face of the whole earth." Genesis 11:9

Pray It! God, help me to always follow You and Your ways.

Explore It! Why couldn't the people finish the great tower? What does it mean to follow God?

Abram and His Family Follow God

What's missing?

Missing: supplies on animals' backs

Abram and His Family Follow God

Genesis 12:1–10, 13, 15:2, 16:1, 18:11

Abram and his wife Sarai were old. They were sad because they did not have any children.

Abram loved God with all of his heart. One day, God said to Abram, "Leave your country and your father's family. Go to a new land that I will show you."

God promised Abram, "I will bless you. I will make your name great. You will be a blessing to others."

Abram listened to God. He and Sarai packed everything that they had. They traveled a long way and stayed in many places. Their nephew Lot went with them.

Abram became very rich with gold, silver, and herds of animals. His nephew Lot also had many animals. There was not enough food and water for all of them. Abram told Lot, "We can share the land. You can choose your land first." Lot was selfish and chose the best land for himself.

Abram was not worried. He knew that God would keep His promises. After Lot moved to his land, God said to Abram, "I will give you all of the land that you see. I will give it to you and to all of your children."

Now, Abram and Sarai knew that they would have children. They built an altar to honor God.

Say It!   "I will make you into a great nation and I will bless you; I will make your name great, and you will be a blessing." Genesis 12:2

Pray It!   Thank You, God, for keeping Your promises.

Explore It! Who chose the best land? What is one example of a selfish choice that you made?

God's Promise to Abram

What's missing?

Missing: stars

God's Promise to Abram

Genesis 15:1–6, 17:1–18, 18:10–15, 21:1–6

God made a promise to Abram. He promised to give him a son. God told Abram, "Look at the heavens and count the stars, if you can. Your family will grow. There will be more children than there are stars in the sky." Abram believed Him.

God changed Abram's name to Abraham, which means *father of many*. God changed Sarai's name to Sarah. "She will be the mother of nations," God said.

When Abraham was 99 years old, God appeared to him. He said, "This time next year, Sarah will have a son." Sarah heard what God had said and laughed. She thought that she was too old to have a baby.

God then said to Abraham, "Why did Sarah laugh? Is anything too hard for the Lord? I will return to you in one year, and Sarah will have a son."

God kept his promise to Abraham and Sarah. One year later, God gave them a son. Abraham and Sarah named the boy Isaac, meaning *laughter*.

"God has brought me laughter," said Sarah. "Let all who hear about this laugh with me."

Say It!   "'Is anything too hard for the Lord?'" Genesis 18:14
Pray It!   Lord, I am thankful that You can do impossible things.
Explore It! What does the name *Abraham* mean? Has God ever done something in your life that seemed impossible? What was it?

Two Different Brothers

What's missing?

Missing: tents

Two Different Brothers

Genesis 25:19–28, 28

When Isaac was 60 years old, his wife Rebekah had twin sons. They named the first son Esau. His body was covered with hair. They named the second son Jacob.

When the boys grew up, Esau became a skilled hunter. He liked to be outside. Jacob was a quiet man who did not like the outdoors. He stayed at home near the tents.

Esau did not get along well with his brother Jacob. Isaac and Rebekah were not happy that their sons argued all of the time. Isaac and Rebekah wanted to help Jacob.

One day, Isaac called Jacob to come to him. He told Jacob to go to his uncle's village to find a wife. Isaac said, "May the mighty God bless you and give you many children. When you come back, you can take over the land where you live now."

Jacob obeyed his father and started on his journey. He prayed that God would keep him safe and bless his life.

Say It!   "'. . . I am the God of your father Abraham. Do not be afraid, for I am with you; I will bless you.'" Genesis 26:24

Pray It!   Lord, thank You for blessing me.

Explore It!   What did Isaac do to help Jacob? Have you ever had a problem getting along with someone? How did you solve it?

A Stairway to Heaven

What's missing?

Missing: stairway to heaven

A Stairway to Heaven

Genesis 28:10–22

Jacob's trip to his uncle's house took a long time. When the sun set, Jacob decided to rest for the night. He found a stone, placed it under his head, and slept. That night, Jacob had a dream. He saw stairs resting on the ground with a top that reached heaven. Angels walked up and down the stairway. Then, Jacob heard a voice. It was God!

"I am the God of Abraham and the God of your father Isaac," God said. "I made a promise to them, and I am making a promise to you today. You will return to this land one day, and you will have a large family. They will spread out across the earth."

God told Jacob, "I am with you. I will watch over you everywhere you go. I will not leave you."

When Jacob woke up, he said, "This must be the house of God. This is the gate of heaven!"

Jacob built an altar starting with the stone he had slept on. Jacob prayed, "If God will take care of me and bring me home safely, then the Lord will be my God."

Jacob left the stone altar as a reminder of God's promise to him and of his promise to God.

Say It! "'I am with you and will watch over you wherever you go.'" Genesis 28:15

Pray It! Thank You, God, for taking care of me.

Explore It! What did Jacob see in his dream? What do you think heaven looks like?

Brothers and Friends

What's missing?

Missing: animals sent by Jacob

Brothers and Friends

Genesis 31:3, 31:17–18, 32:3–32, 33:1–4

Jacob lived with his uncle for a long time. God blessed Jacob with a large family and many animals. God told Jacob, "Go back to your father's land. I will be with you."

Jacob was worried. He had not seen his brother Esau in many years. He wondered if Esau still did not like him.

Jacob gathered his family and his belongings. They began the trip. They set up camp close to Jacob's father's house. Jacob sent messengers to tell Esau that he wanted to be friends. The messengers returned and said, "Your brother is coming to meet you with 400 men!" Jacob was afraid, so he prayed to God for help.

Jacob sent goats, camels, cows, bulls, and donkeys as gifts to Esau. Jacob also sent his family ahead of him.

Jacob was alone in camp. During the night, a man came out of the darkness and began wrestling with Jacob. Jacob fought with the man all night. Finally, the man said, "Let me go. It is morning."

Jacob answered, "I will not let you go until you bless me."

The man said, "I am changing your name to Israel because you have fought with God and man, and you have won!" Jacob knew that the man was God, and that God had let him live.

The next day, Jacob walked to Esau's house. Jacob bowed to Esau. Esau ran to Jacob and hugged him. Jacob and Esau were friends! Jacob knew that God had been kind to him.

Say It! "'. . . God has been gracious to me and I have all I need.'" Genesis 33:11

Pray It! Heavenly Father, thank You for giving me what I need.

Explore It! What new name did God give to Jacob? Many names have meanings. Do you know what your name means?

A New Coat and Big Dreams

What's missing?

Missing: designs and colors on coat

A New Coat and Big Dreams

Genesis 35:18, 35:23–26, 37:1–11

Jacob had 12 sons that he loved very much. Joseph was the 11th son. When Joseph was 17 years old, Jacob made him a beautiful coat of many colors. Joseph was very proud of his coat. Joseph's brothers were mean to him because they did not have fancy coats like Joseph's.

One night, Joseph had a dream. He dreamed that he and his brothers were working in a field and putting wheat into bundles. Joseph saw his bundle of wheat stand. All of his brothers' bundles of wheat bowed to it.

Joseph was excited about his dream. He told his brothers that he did not know what the dream meant. His brothers wondered, "Do you think that Joseph will rule over us?" They were not happy about Joseph's dream.

Joseph had another dream. It was like the first one. In this dream, Joseph saw the sun, the moon, and 11 stars bowing to him.

Joseph told his father about the dream. His father wondered, "Will your mother, your brothers, and I bow in front of you one day?" No one knew what these dreams meant.

Say It! "'The land I gave to Abraham and Isaac I also give to you.'" Genesis 35:12

Pray It! God, help me not to be jealous of what others have.

Explore It! What did Jacob give to Joseph? Have you ever been jealous of someone? Why?

Joseph Helps His Brothers

What's missing?

Missing: sacks of grain

Joseph Helps His Brothers

Genesis 37:12, 37:31–33, 41:25–41, 42–43, 45–46, 47:11–12, 50:20

One day, Joseph was tending the flocks. He did not come home. For many years, his father Jacob thought that a wild animal had killed Joseph. But, Joseph was not dead. He was living in a palace in Egypt! He was an officer of the king.

Joseph told the king that soon people would not have enough food. The king began to save food for the people of Egypt. When people everywhere became hungry, Egypt had food to share.

Joseph's father sent 10 of his sons to Egypt to buy food. The youngest son, Benjamin, stayed home. The brothers entered the palace. They bowed to Joseph. They did not know that Joseph was their brother, but he recognized them. The dreams that Joseph had many years ago came true. His brothers were bowing to him.

Joseph gave sacks of food to his brothers. He said, "One brother must stay here until you bring Benjamin to me."

Joseph waited until Benjamin and his brothers returned. Then, Joseph told his brothers who he was.

The brothers were afraid because they had been mean to Joseph when he was young. Joseph said, "Don't be afraid. You did something bad, but God turned it into something good. God brought me here to help the hungry people."

Then, Joseph sent for his father. The whole family was together in Egypt.

Say It!   "'So then, it was not you who sent me here, but God.'" Genesis 45:8

Pray It!   Lord, lead me to places where I can help others.

Explore It!   Why wasn't Joseph angry with his brothers? Have you forgiven someone for being mean to you?

A Baby in a Basket

What's missing?

Missing: basket

A Baby in a Basket

Exodus 1, 2:1–5

God's promise to Jacob came true. Jacob's family was large. They spread out across the earth. They were the Israelites.

The new king of Egypt was worried. He thought that the Israelites were too powerful. The king told his soldiers to make the Israelites slaves. The soldiers treated the Israelites badly. They made the Israelites work very hard.

Israelite families continued to grow. So, the king gave another order. He told his soldiers that every Israelite baby boy must die.

One Israelite mother created a plan to save her son. She hid him from the soldiers. She put him in a basket and covered it. She carefully placed it in the tall grass of the Nile River.

She told her daughter, Miriam, "Stay close to your baby brother, and see what happens to him." Soon, Miriam saw the king's daughter walking toward the river. The king's daughter saw the covered basket!

Say It! "The Lord said, 'I have indeed seen the misery of my people in Egypt. I have heard them crying out.'" Exodus 3:7

Pray It! Thank You, God, for protecting me.

Explore It! How did the mother of Moses save his life? Can you think of a time when God protected you from danger? Talk about it.

His Name Is Moses

Who's missing?

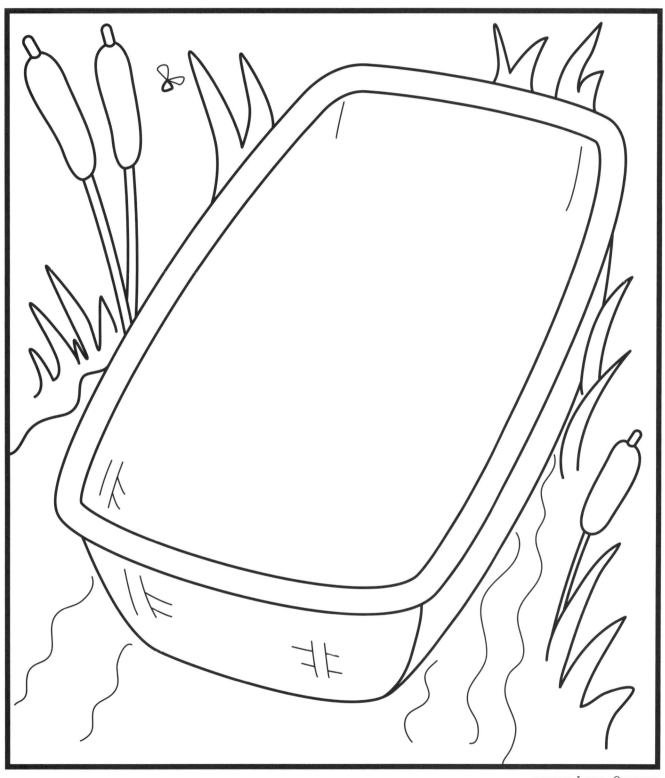

Missing: Baby Moses

His Name Is Moses

Exodus 2:5–10

The king's daughter lived in the royal palace. She was a princess. One day, she went to the Nile River to take a bath. She noticed a basket in the tall grass. When the princess opened the basket, a baby began to cry. She held him close.

"This must be one of the Israelite babies," she said. She knew that her father was angry at the Israelites. She knew that Israelite baby boys were in danger.

The baby's sister, Miriam, was hiding close by. She and her mother had put the baby there to keep him safe from the king's soldiers.

Miriam walked up to the princess. She asked the princess, "Should I get someone to take care of the baby for you?"

"Yes," the princess said. Miriam came back with her own mother. The princess said, "Take care of this baby and feed him. I will pay you for your help. When he is older and stronger, return him to me."

The baby's mother was happy to take care of him. When the baby grew, she gave him to the princess. The princess said, "I will name him Moses because I lifted him out of the water."

Say It! ". . . She named him Moses, saying, 'I drew him out of the water.'" Exodus 2:10

Pray It! Lord, I thank You for always doing what is best for me.

Explore It! What name did the king's daughter give to the baby boy? Have you ever been brave like Miriam and her mother?

The Burning Bush

What's missing?

Missing: flames on bush

The Burning Bush

Exodus 3:1–12

When Moses grew up, he left the palace where he lived and became a shepherd. A new king ruled over Egypt, but the Israelites were still slaves. God wanted to help them.

One day, Moses was taking care of a flock of sheep near a mountain. He saw a bush that was on fire. Flames covered the bush, but it was not burned. Moses had never seen anything like it. When he walked closer to the bush, a voice called to him.

"Moses! Moses!" the voice said. "I am the God of your father, the God of Abraham, Isaac, and Jacob. Take off your sandals. This is holy ground." Moses hid his face because he was afraid to look at God.

God said, "I have seen the suffering of My people in Egypt. I have come to help them. Tell the king to let My people go. You will lead them to a better place. It is a land flowing with milk and honey."

Moses did not think that he could do what God had asked. He did not think that the king would listen to him.

God told Moses, "I will be with you. Everyone will know that I have sent you. You will bring My people out of Egypt. All of you will worship Me on this mountain."

Say It!   "'. . . When you have brought the people out of Egypt, you will worship God on this mountain.'" Exodus 3:12

Pray It!   Lord, I give You thanks for always leading me in the right direction.

Explore It!   What did God tell Moses to do with his sandals? Describe a time when God helped you do something that was really difficult.

Moses the Messenger

What's missing?

Missing: king's headdress and throne

Moses the Messenger

Exodus 4:27, 5, 6:1

God sent Moses' brother, Aaron, to meet Moses at the mountain. They traveled to Egypt to tell the king what God said. When they met with the king, Moses said, "God commands you to let His people go."

The king did not care. He said, "Who is this God? I do not know this God, so I will not obey him. I will not free the Israelites."

Moses replied, "If you do not let the Israelites go, God will bring terrible things to Egypt." The king did not care. He made God's people work harder. He would not give them the supplies that they needed to do their jobs.

The Israelites became angry with Moses and Aaron. They blamed the brothers for their punishment. Moses was very upset.

He asked God, "Did you send me to make life more difficult for Your people? You have not rescued them as You promised."

God answered Moses, "Watch what I will do to the king. He will see My powerful hand. Then, he will let the people of Israel go."

Say It! ". . . This is what the Lord, the God of Israel, says: 'Let my people go.'" Exodus 5:1

Pray It! Dear God, help me to always obey You even when it seems difficult.

Explore It! Who did Moses take with him to see the king? The king didn't know God. How do people get to know God?

Frogs, Bugs, Hail, and More!

What should there be more of in this picture?

Missing: more frogs

Frogs, Bugs, Hail, and More!

Exodus 7:1–13, 8–11:1

The king of Egypt did not believe in God's power. He refused to free the Israelites from slavery. God spoke to Moses and Moses' brother, Aaron. He told them to perform a miracle for the king. Moses and Aaron did what God said. Aaron threw his staff on the ground in front of the king. The staff became a snake. But, the king would not free the Israelites.

Moses and Aaron returned to the king many times. Each time the king refused to let the Israelites leave Egypt. Aaron raised his staff over the land, and God covered the country with frogs. The king agreed to let the Israelites go if Moses got rid of the frogs. Moses asked God to remove the frogs. The king still would not free God's people.

God sent swarms of biting gnats. Later, he sent swarms of flies. Still, the king said, "No! I will not let the people go." God caused the Egyptians' farm animals to get sick. Next, dust fell from the sky, causing sores on the skin of the Egyptians. But, the king did not change his mind.

God told Moses to lift his hand to the sky. Rain, thunder, and hail came. It was the worst storm in history, ruining the land and plants in Egypt. Next, God covered the land with locusts. The insects ate all of the plants that were left after the hail. Then, God made the sky dark for three days. The king would not let the Israelites go.

God told Moses, "I will do one more thing to the king and to Egypt. After that, he will let you and your people go."

Say It!   "The Lord had said to Moses, 'Pharaoh will refuse to listen to you—so that my wonders may be multiplied in Egypt.'" Exodus 11:9

Pray It!   Thank You, Lord, for being such a powerful and righteous God.

Explore It!   Which bad thing happened first? Tell about a time when it was hard to change someone's mind.

The King Changes His Mind

What's missing?

Missing: marks on house

The King Changes His Mind

Exodus 11, 12:12–37

God told Moses to give the king one last warning. He said, "Tell the king that if he does not let God's people go, the oldest child and the oldest animal in every family will die. Even the king's own son will die."

This warning did not change the king's mind. The angry king still said, "No!"

God wanted to keep the Israelite children safe. He gave His instructions to Moses and Aaron. He told them to warn every Israelite family.

Moses and Aaron told the Israelites, "Mark the tops and sides of your doors. When God searches in the night, He will see the marks on your doors. He will know that you are His people. He will pass over your houses, and He will not harm anyone inside."

At midnight, the Egyptians cried because someone died in every Egyptian family. The king called for Moses. He said to Moses, "Get out of here! You and all of the Israelites, leave my people! Worship the Lord, just as you have asked. Take your flocks and herds, and give me your blessing."

God softened the hearts of the Egyptians. They gave gold, silver, and clothing to the Israelites. Then, God led Moses, Aaron, and the Israelites out of Egypt.

Say It!   "And on that very day the Lord brought the Israelites out of Egypt." Exodus 12:51

Pray It!   Dear God, help me to always remember how You saved Your people.

Explore It!   What did the Israelites do to save their oldest children? Can you think of a time when God made someone's heart kinder?

A Cloud and Fire Lead the Way

What's missing?

Missing: column of cloud

A Cloud and Fire Lead the Way

Exodus 13:17–22, 14:1–20

God led Moses, Aaron, and the Israelites out of Egypt. During the day, God guided His people in a special way. He stayed ahead of them in a cloud shaped like a tall column. At night, He showed them the way with a tall column of fire that gave them light. The cloud and the fire helped the people travel during the day and night.

The king of Egypt was angry about his decision. He said to his soldiers, "What have we done? We let the Israelites go, and now we have no one to do our work!" The king went with his soldiers and his chariots to capture the Israelites and force them to come back to Egypt.

The Israelites were camping by the sea when they saw the soldiers with their horses and chariots. The Israelites were frightened, and they cried out to God. They asked Moses, "Why did you bring us here to die? We wish we were still slaves in Egypt."

Moses answered the Israelites. He said, "Do not be afraid. God will save you. He will fight for you."

That night, the cloud came between the armies of Egypt and Israel. It brought darkness to the king's army. They could not see the Israelites in the dark. So, the Israelites were safe all night.

Say It! "'. . . Do not be afraid. Stand firm and you will see the deliverance the Lord will bring you today.'" Exodus 14:13
Pray It! Thank You, God, for leading the way.
Explore It! How did God lead the Israelites during the day? When have you trusted God even when things were not going well?

A Path Through the Red Sea

What's missing?

Missing: walls of water with path in middle

A Path Through the Red Sea

Exodus 14:15–31

The Israelites camped near the Red Sea. The Egyptian king and his army were nearby with their horses and chariots. They were ready to fight the Israelites. They wanted to take the Israelites back to Egypt.

But, the Egyptian king and his army could not see the Israelites. God had placed a column of cloud in front of the Egyptians. They did not go near the Israelites that night.

God spoke to Moses. He said, "Why are the people of Israel crying out to me? Tell them to move on. Hold out your staff. Reach out your hand toward the Red Sea. I will make a path through the sea. Then, the people can cross the sea on dry ground."

Moses did what God told him, and a path appeared through the middle of the sea! The Israelites began walking across dry land with a wall of water on each side of them.

The Egyptian soldiers, horses, and chariots chased the Israelites. The chariots moved slowly because God made their wheels fall off.

When the last Israelite had crossed the Red Sea, God told Moses to raise his staff over the water. Moses obeyed God, and the sea covered the Egyptians.

The Israelites knew that God had saved them. They praised God and trusted Him. They also trusted Moses.

Say It! ". . . The waters were divided, and the Israelites went through the sea on dry ground with a wall of water on their right and on their left." Exodus 14:21–22

Pray It! Dear God, we praise You for answering prayers.

Explore It! How did the Israelites get away from the Egyptian army? How do you take time to praise God when He helps you?

Manna from Heaven

What should there be more of in this picture?

Missing: more manna

Manna from Heaven

Exodus 15:22–27, 16:1–30

Moses and the Israelites walked for a long time in the hot, dry desert. They were very thirsty. They came to a place with water, but the water tasted bitter. God told Moses to throw a piece of wood into the water. Moses threw the piece of wood into the water, and the water became sweet. The people had water to drink, and they were happy.

Soon, the people complained again. "We're hungry. We have no food to eat. We should have stayed in Egypt. We had food there."

God heard His people's cries. He told Moses, "I will send bread from heaven. The people will know that I brought them from Egypt and that I will take care of them."

The next morning, the people saw that thin flakes had fallen everywhere. It looked like frost on the ground. The people called the bread *manna*.

Moses told the people, "God will send manna every morning. Take only what you need. Eat all of the bread. Do not save any for the next day. On the sixth day, gather enough to eat for two days. On Sunday, you must rest."

Each day, God sent manna. Most people took only what they needed. On the sixth day, the people gathered enough manna to last for two days so that on the seventh day they could rest.

Say It! "Then the Lord said to Moses, 'I will rain down bread from heaven for you.'" Exodus 16:4

Pray It! We are thankful to You, Father, for the good food You give us.

Explore It! What kind of food did God send from heaven? How do you thank God for your food before you eat?

Water from a Rock

What's missing?

Missing: water pouring from the rock

Water from a Rock

Exodus 17:1–6

The Israelites continued to travel across the desert. They stopped to set up camp, but there was no water. The people were angry and told Moses that they were thirsty. They said, "Give us water to drink!"

Moses answered, "Why do you yell at me? Why do you want to test God?"

But the people were angry with Moses. They asked him, "Why did you bring us out of Egypt? Did you want us, our children, and our animals to die of thirst?"

Moses asked God what he should do. God said, "Carry your wooden staff, and take a few men with you. Walk ahead of the men until you reach the large rock. I will be there. Hit the rock with your staff."

The men watched Moses walk to the rock and hit it with his staff. Water came out of the rock. There was enough water for every person and animal to drink.

Say It! "'. . . Strike the rock, and water will come out of it for the people to drink.'" Exodus 17:6

Pray It! Lord, help me trust in You for everything I need.

Explore It! Why do you think that God wanted Moses to take a few men with him to the rock? Have you ever worried about something when you didn't need to?

The Ten Commandments

What's missing?

Missing: stone tablets

Missing: stone tablets

The Ten Commandments

Exodus 19, 20:1–17, 31:18, 32:15–16

The Israelites arrived at Mount Sinai three months after they left Egypt. God said to Moses, "Tell My people that I led them out of Egypt because they are My holy nation. But, they must follow My rules, My commandments. In three days, they should meet Me at the bottom of this mountain."

Moses gathered the people at the bottom of the mountain. The mountain shook, and the people heard a trumpet. They saw smoke rising from the mountain. God told Moses to climb the mountain.

When Moses reached the top of the mountain, God explained the Ten Commandments to him. Later, God wrote the commandments on stone tablets. Moses carried the tablets down the mountain to share with the Israelites.

"God promises that He will bless you if you follow His rules," Moses explained. Moses read the Ten Commandments to the people.

1. Love God more than you love anyone else.
2. Don't make anything in your life more important than God.
3. Always say God's name with love and respect.
4. Honor the Lord by resting on Sunday.
5. Love and respect your mom and dad.
6. Never hurt anyone.
7. Always be faithful to your husband or wife.
8. Don't take anything that isn't yours.
9. Always tell the truth.
10. Be happy with what you have. Don't wish for other people's things.

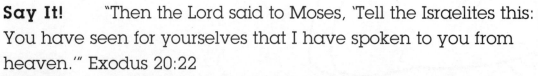

Say It! "Then the Lord said to Moses, 'Tell the Israelites this: You have seen for yourselves that I have spoken to you from heaven.'" Exodus 20:22

Pray It! Thank You, God, for giving me rules to help me make good choices.

Explore It! What did God promise if the people followed His rules? Why should you obey rules?

God's Covenant

What's missing?

Missing: angel on end of box

God's Covenant

Exodus 32:30, 34, 35:22–29, 37:1–9, 40:34–38; Numbers 10:33–34

The Israelites broke God's rules. They did not follow the Ten Commandments. God told Moses to cut two new stones. God wanted to write His commandments again.

God came in a cloud and spoke to the Israelites. He said, "I do not get angry quickly. I am full of love. I forgive everyone who does not obey me."

God made a new promise to His people. Moses wrote the commandments on the new stone tablets. God spoke to Moses again. God wanted the people to build a holy tent. He called the tent a tabernacle. The people could pray to God in the tent.

Moses told the people, "This is what the Lord wants you to do. You should do your work in six days. You must rest on the seventh day."

The Israelites used gold, silver, and jewels to decorate God's tent. Some workers made beautiful tables and altars. Other workers used red, purple, and blue yarn to make curtains.

God wanted a special box for His promises. The box is called the ark of the covenant because a covenant is a promise.

A worker made the box from wood and decorated it with a gold angel on each end. He made two poles to carry the box.

The people finished the work. They began traveling again. Each day, God came in a cloud over the tent. When the cloud went away, the people traveled. At night, God sent a tall column of fire. It guarded the people when they rested. The cloud stayed with the Israelites everywhere they traveled.

Say It!   "'. . . I am making a covenant with you. Before all your people I will do wonders never before done in any nation in all the world. The people you live among will see how awesome is the work that I, the Lord, will do for you.'" Exodus 34:10

Pray It!   Help me, Father, to always remember Your covenant.

Explore It!   Why did God tell Moses to cut out two new stones? Describe a time when you did something wrong and you were forgiven.

The Land of Milk and Honey

What's missing?

Missing: fruit hanging from pole

The Land of Milk and Honey

Numbers 13, 14:1–9, 14:30

After a long time, the Israelites arrived at the border of Canaan. This was the land that God promised them. The Israelites set up camp.

God told Moses to send 12 leaders to look at the land. They saw the soil, trees, plants, and fruit. They studied the cities and towns. After 40 days, the men came back to the camp. They carried a pole between them. The fruit that they had gathered hung from the pole.

The men said, "We went where you asked us to go. The soil there grows many fruits and vegetables. It is the land of milk and honey! But, the people who live there are strong and powerful. The cities are large and have high walls around them."

Some of the 12 leaders told stories about the land that were not true. They said, "The land that we saw is not good. It will destroy the people who live on it. The people there are so tall that we look like grasshoppers next to them." These men were afraid. They did not think that God would help them. God told Moses that He would not let these men come into the land of milk and honey.

Two leaders, Joshua and Caleb, believed that God would help them. They said, "We are not afraid! Those people are strong, but God is stronger! The Lord is with us."

God told Moses, "Caleb follows me with his heart." Then, God blessed Joshua, Caleb, and their children.

Say It! "If the Lord is pleased with us, He will lead us into that land, a land flowing with milk and honey, and will give it to us.'" Numbers 14:8

Pray It! We praise You, God, for always taking care of us.

Explore It! Why weren't Caleb and Joshua afraid? Describe a time when you trusted God to take care of you.

Rahab Helps God's People

What's missing?

Missing: red rope on window

Rahab Helps God's People

Joshua 1:1–2, 2:1–23

After Moses died, God told Joshua to lead the Israelites into the promised land. Joshua wanted to learn more about the land, especially Jericho. So, he sent two spies to Jericho.

The king of Jericho knew that the spies were in the city. He heard that they were hiding at a woman's house. The king sent his soldiers to see the woman. Her name was Rahab.

Rahab knew that God had promised the land to the Israelites. She knew that God had parted the Red Sea for them. Rahab hid the spies, and the king's soldiers could not find them.

"I know that your God is powerful," Rahab told Joshua's spies. "When your army captures Jericho, will you be kind to my family since I have been kind to you?"

The spies said, "Yes. Bring your family inside your house. Then, hang a short, red rope from your window. Our army will see the rope, and they will know that you are God's friend."

The spies left Rahab's house. They camped in the hills for three days until the king's soldiers stopped looking for them. Then, they went back to Joshua and told him everything that had happened.

Say It!   "'. . . the Lord your God is God in heaven above and on the earth below.'" Joshua 2:11

Pray It!   Thank You, God, for saving me.

Explore It!   What kind of help did Rahab ask the spies for? Describe a time when God used you to help others.

The Walls of Jericho Fall

What's missing?

Missing: trumpets

The Walls of Jericho Fall

Joshua 6

The people of Jericho shut their gates tightly. They guarded the walls of the city. They knew that Joshua and the Israelites wanted to get in. Joshua was near Jericho when God spoke to him.

God said, "I am giving Jericho to you. I will give its king and his army to you too." God told Joshua His plan to win Jericho.

God told Joshua, "Each day, march once around the city with your men. Do this for six days. Carry the ark of the covenant in front of you.

"Seven priests should walk with you and blow trumpets. On the seventh day, the army and the priests should march seven times around the city. The priests should blow their trumpets. Tell the army to shout when they hear the trumpets blast. Then, the walls of the city will fall. You will go straight in."

Joshua told the plan to his men. When they shouted on the seventh day, the walls of Jericho fell. The Israelites rushed into Jericho and took over the city.

Joshua and his army kept their promise to Rahab. She had believed in the power of God. She had helped Joshua by hiding his spies, so Joshua and his army saved Rahab and her family. God blessed Joshua.

Say It!   "Then the Lord said to Joshua, 'See, I have delivered Jericho into your hands, along with its king and its fighting men.'" Joshua 6:2

Pray It!   Lord, we are thankful that You always have a plan.

Explore It!   Which sound made the walls of Jericho fall? What do you think is God's plan for your life?

Deborah's Army

What's missing?

Missing: rain and clouds

Deborah's Army

Judges 4–5

The Israelites were not following God's rules, and He was not happy. God let a mean king rule the Israelites for 20 years. The Israelites prayed to God for help.

Deborah was an Israelite leader and a judge. God told her how to help God's people. Deborah went to a man named Barak and said, "God wants you to help the people of Israel. You must lead an army against the king."

Barak said, "I will go if you go with me." So, Deborah and Barak gathered 10,000 men. But, the king had a bigger army and 900 chariots. Deborah knew that God's power would help the Israelites win.

When the battle started, the earth shook and rain poured. All of the king's chariots started sinking in the mud. The Israelites circled around the chariots and won the battle. Barak and Deborah sang a song to thank God for His help.

Say It! "'. . . I will sing to the Lord, I will sing; I will make music to the Lord, the God of Israel.'" Judges 5:3

Pray It! Thank You, God, for helping me.

Explore It! What jobs did Deborah have before God asked her to lead an army? Name a brave woman that you know.

God Chooses a Boy

What's missing?

Missing: water in stream

God Chooses a Boy

Judges 6:1–16, 7:1–7

The Israelites broke God's commandments again. They worshipped other gods. God sent mean people to rule the Israelites. They took the Israelites' animals and destroyed their crops.

The Israelites hid in caves. They prayed, "God, please help us! We are hungry and afraid!"

God heard His people's prayers. God sent an angel to a boy named Gideon. The angel said to Gideon, "The Lord is with you."

God told Gideon, "You are strong. I am sending you to save Israel."

Gideon asked, "How can I save Israel? My family is small. I am the youngest."

God answered, "I will be with you."

Gideon listened to God. He gathered a large army. God thought that Gideon had too many soldiers. God said, "I do not need a large army to win. I want a small army so that people will know that I saved them."

Gideon spoke God's words to the men. He said, "Anyone who is afraid can go home." About 22,000 men left, and 10,000 stayed.

God said, "There are still too many men. Take them to the stream to drink water. Keep the men who drink water from their hands. Send away the men who drink from the stream like dogs."

Only 300 men drank from their hands. God said to Gideon, "I will use these 300 men, and I will save you."

Say It!   "When the angel of the Lord appeared to Gideon, he said, 'The Lord is with you, mighty warrior.'" Judges 6:12

Pray It!   We are blessed, Lord, that You are such a big God.

Explore It!   How many men were in Gideon's final army? Tell about a time when you were able to do something with God's help.

A Battle Without a Fight

What's missing?

Missing: jar with torch inside

A Battle Without a Fight

Judges 7:8–22

Gideon had 300 men in his army. God promised Gideon that his men would win the battle against their enemy.

That night, God sent Gideon and his servant to look at the enemy's camp. Gideon saw so many soldiers that they looked like insects. The number of camels was like the number of grains of sand on a beach.

Gideon came back to his army and followed God's plan. He divided the 300 men into three smaller armies. He gave each man a trumpet and a jar with a torch in it. He told them, "Follow me, and do exactly what I do."

Gideon and his 100 men reached the edge of the enemy's camp. They blew their trumpets and broke their jars. They yelled, "For the Lord and for Gideon!" Then, the other 200 men did the same thing.

The enemies heard the noise. It sounded like Gideon's army was bigger than theirs. The enemies were confused and started to fight each other.

Gideon and his men watched their enemies run away. Gideon and the Israelites won the battle without fighting.

Say It!   "When I and all who are with me blow our trumpets, then from all around the camp blow yours and shout, 'For the Lord and for Gideon!'" Judges 7:18

Pray It!   Father in Heaven, please help me to follow Your special plan for me.

Explore It!   What did the Israelites shout? Why does God give us exact directions to follow?

Young Samson Grows Strong

What's missing?

Missing: lion

Young Samson Grows Strong

Judges 13–15

When the Israelites did not obey God again, He put the Philistines in charge of them. The Philistines were mean to the Israelites for 40 years.

God sent an angel to an Israelite woman. The angel said, "You will have a son. He will save God's people from the Philistines. Your son will be different from other children. Do not cut his hair, and he will work for God in a special way. Your son will help Israel against the Philistines."

The woman told her husband what the angel said. The baby was born, and his parents named him Samson. They never cut his hair. Samson grew much stronger than other boys, and the Lord blessed him.

One day, Samson saw a Philistine woman. He told his parents that he wanted to marry her. Samson's parents were sad. They said, "Philistines are not God's people."

But, Samson said, "She is the right one for me." Samson went to the woman's town to talk to her. On the way, a roaring lion attacked him. God gave Samson great strength. Samson fought the young lion with his bare hands. Samson won the fight.

Samson married the Philistine woman. She was not a good wife for Samson. She did many things against him and against God. But, God wanted things to happen that way. It was part of His plan to help the Israelites.

Say It! ". . . No razor may be used on his head, because the boy is to be . . . set apart to God from birth." Judges 13:5

Pray It! Father in heaven, thank You for hearing our prayers.

Explore It! What kind of animal attacked Samson? Describe a time when you tried to do things your own way instead of God's way.

God Makes Samson Strong Again

What's missing?

Missing: columns of the temple

God Makes Samson Strong Again

Judges 16:2–31

Samson was an Israelite leader for 20 years. The Philistines did not like Samson because he was stronger than other men. They did not know that Samson's long hair made him strong.

Samson knew a Philistine woman named Delilah. Samson told Delilah a secret. He told her that his long hair made him strong. Samson trusted Delilah, but she tricked him. She told the secret to the Philistines. They cut Samson's hair while he was sleeping.

When Samson woke up, he was not strong anymore. The Philistines captured him. They put heavy chains around Samson. They blinded him and locked him in jail. Samson's hair began to grow again.

More than 3,000 Philistines gathered for a party. The guards took Samson out of jail to show him to the crowd. A man led Samson by the hand. Samson asked the man, "Will you let me lean on the columns of the temple?"

The man led Samson to the columns. Samson prayed, "God, please make me strong one more time." God answered his prayer. Samson pushed the columns apart, and the temple fell on Samson and the 3,000 Philistines.

Say It! ". . . Then he pushed with all his might, and down came the temple on the rulers and all the people in it." Judges 16:30

Pray It! Lord, thank You for being strong when I am weak.

Explore It! What was the secret reason that Samson was so strong? Delilah wasn't loyal. What does it mean to be loyal?

Friends for Life

What's missing?

Missing: "Moab" on sign pointing left, "Israel" on sign pointing right

Friends for Life

Ruth 1:1–19, 2:10–12, 4:13–17

There was not enough food in Israel, so some people moved to other places. Naomi and her husband moved their family to Moab. Naomi's husband died, and she stayed in Moab with her two sons. Her sons married Moab women named Ruth and Orpah. Ten years later, Naomi's sons died.

Naomi heard that Israel had food again. She told Ruth and Orpah, "I am going home to Israel. You should go back to your mothers' homes. You can meet new husbands there."

Ruth and Orpah did not want to go, but Naomi said that it was best for everyone. Orpah kissed Naomi good–bye, but Ruth would not leave Naomi. Ruth said, "Where you go, I will go. Where you stay, I will stay. Your people are my people, and your God is my God."

Naomi and Ruth went to Bethlehem together. The people welcomed Ruth because she was Naomi's friend. God blessed Ruth for her kindness to Naomi. Ruth married and had a son named Obed. Obed was the father of Jesse. Jesse had a son named David. When David grew up, God chose him to be king.

Say It!　"'Where you go I will go; where you stay I will stay. Your people will be my people and your God my God.'" Ruth 1:16

Pray It!　Lord, help me to be a true friend.

Explore It!　Who went with Naomi back to Israel? What has a good friend done to show you friendship?

God Calls Samuel

What's missing?

Missing: moon and stars

God Calls Samuel

1 Samuel 3:1–10, 3:19–21

Eli was an old priest. His eyes were weak, and he could not see well. A boy named Samuel helped him. Samuel stayed with Eli in the temple at night.

One night, a voice called, "Samuel!"

Samuel ran to Eli's room and said, "Here I am. You called me."

Eli said, "I did not call you. Go back to your room and lie down."

Samuel heard the voice call "Samuel!" again. He got up from his bed and went to Eli's room. Again, Eli told Samuel that he did not call him.

Samuel did not know that God was calling him. The third time that this happened, Eli told Samuel what to do next. He told Samuel to say, "Speak, Lord. I am listening."

Samuel did just as Eli had told him. After that night, God spoke to Samuel many times.

God was with Samuel as he grew up. God helped Samuel know things before they happened. Everyone knew that Samuel was a man of God.

Say It! "The Lord came and stood there, calling as at the other times, 'Samuel! Samuel!' Then Samuel said, 'Speak, for your servant is listening.'" 1 Samuel 3:10

Pray It! Thank You, God, for calling me to be your servant.

Explore It! Who did Samuel think was calling his name? How can you be a servant of God?

The Boy King

What's missing?

Missing: oil dripping from horn

The Boy King

1 Samuel 16:1–13

Samuel was a wise man. God told him how to help people, even kings.

God was ready to choose a new king for Israel. He told Samuel, "I am sending you to Bethlehem. I have chosen one of Jesse's sons to be king."

Samuel had a ram's horn that he filled with oil. He used the oil to bless the people. God told Samuel, "Bring your horn. Fill it with oil to bless the new king."

Samuel went to Bethlehem. Jesse brought one of his sons to Samuel. But, God told Samuel, "I have not chosen this son. I do not care how people look on the outside. I look at what is in their hearts."

Jesse brought six other sons to Samuel, but God did not choose them either. Samuel asked, "Do you have other sons?"

Jesse answered, "I have one more. David is my youngest son. He is taking care of my sheep."

Samuel said, "Bring him to me."

David walked into the house. God told Samuel, "He is the one. He will be the next king of Israel."

Samuel blessed David with oil. The spirit of God came to David and gave him power.

Say It! "'. . . The Lord does not look at the things man looks at. Man looks at the outward appearance, but the Lord looks at the heart.'" 1 Samuel 16:7

Pray It! Father, I am blessed that You always see the best in me.

Explore It! Which of Jesse's sons did Samuel choose as the next king of Israel? Have you ever felt like you weren't old enough to help?

David and Goliath

What's missing?

Missing: slingshot and stone

David and Goliath

1 Samuel 17

The Philistines wanted to fight the Israelites. The Israelites lined up for the battle. One Philistine soldier stepped out. He was Goliath, and he was more than nine feet tall. He wore heavy metal armor.

Goliath shouted to the Israelites, "Choose a man to fight me. If he wins, the Philistines will serve the Israelites. If I win, you will serve us." Goliath shouted to the Israelites each day, but they were too afraid to fight Goliath.

On the 40th day, David heard Goliath shout at the Israelite soldiers again. David wanted to fight the giant, but King Saul said, "You are just a boy. You are too young to fight."

David told King Saul that he was a shepherd. Sometimes, wild animals attacked the sheep. David said, "The Lord protected me when I fought lions and bears with my bare hands. The Lord will protect me now." David knew that Samuel had blessed him with God's power.

"Go," said King Saul. "The Lord be with you." King Saul gave David his armor and helmet. David tried to wear them, but they were too heavy. He gave them back to the king.

David gathered five smooth stones from a stream and put them in his bag. He took his slingshot and walked toward Goliath.

Goliath laughed when he saw how small David was. David told Goliath, "You have a spear, but I have God on my side." David took a stone from his bag and slung it at the giant. Goliath fell to the ground. The Philistines saw that their hero was dead, so they ran away. David won the battle!

Say It!   "David said to the Philistine, 'You come against me with sword and spear and javelin, but I come against you in the name of the Lord Almighty.'" 1 Samuel 17:45

Pray It!   Lord, I thank You for being on my side.

Explore It!   What was the name of the Philistine giant? Describe a time when you were afraid and the Lord protected you.

Elijah Helps a Family

What's missing?

Missing: flour and oil containers

Elijah Helps a Family

1 Kings 17:1–16, 17:24

God used Elijah to help the Israelites. He told Elijah what to say to the Israelites. God said that soon there would not be enough water to drink.

God told Elijah to go to a stream. Elijah drank the water there, and the birds fed him each day. There was no rain, so the water dried up.

God told Elijah, "Go to town. You will meet a woman. She will give you food."

Elijah saw the woman gathering sticks. He said, "Will you bring me a piece of bread and some water to drink?"

The woman told Elijah that she had only a little flour in a jar and a little oil in a jug. She and her son would soon have nothing to eat.

Elijah said, "Do not be afraid. Go home and make some bread for me and for your family. God will give you flour and oil until He brings rain again."

The woman went home and made bread. She gave it to Elijah. The woman and her son had food every day. The jar of flour was never empty, and the jug always had oil in it. The woman said to Elijah, "I know that you tell the truth because God speaks through you."

Say It! "For this is what the Lord, the God of Israel, says: 'The jar of flour will not be used up and the jug of oil will not run dry until the day the Lord gives rain on the land.'" 1 Kings 17:14

Pray It! Help me, Father, to be kind to others.

Explore It! What did the woman say when Elijah asked her for food? Have you ever shared with someone even when you did not have much to share?

A Chariot of Fire

What's missing?

Missing: fire

A Chariot of Fire

2 Kings 2:1–15

Elijah had a helper named Elisha. Elisha loved and honored Elijah for many years. Elijah grew old and was ready to go to heaven. God told Elijah that a strong wind would take him to heaven.

Elijah told Elisha, "Stay here. God told me to go to the Jordan River." But, Elisha wanted to walk with him. When they reached the river, 50 men were there.

Elijah rolled up his coat and hit the water with it. The water divided and made a dry path. Elijah and Elisha walked across the river.

Elijah asked Elisha, "What can I do for you before I go to heaven?" Elisha said that he wanted twice the power that God gave to Elijah. Elijah said, "It is yours if you can see me going to heaven."

A chariot of fire and horses of fire came between the men. Elisha watched Elijah go to heaven in a strong wind.

Then, Elisha saw Elijah's coat on the ground. He picked it up and went back to the river. Elisha struck the water with Elijah's coat. The water divided and made a dry path. Elisha walked across the river on dry ground. The 50 men watched and said, "God has blessed Elisha with Elijah's spirit."

Say It! ". . . suddenly a chariot of fire and horses of fire appeared and separated the two of them, and Elijah went up to heaven in a whirlwind." 2 Kings 2:11

Pray It! Thank You, God, for blessing me with Your spirit.

Explore It! How did Elijah go to heaven? Elisha was Elijah's helper. How have you been a helper to others?

Elisha Heals a Man

What's missing?

Missing: water of Jordan River

Elisha Heals a Man

2 Kings 5:1–19

Naaman was a leader of King Aram's army. God helped Naaman win battles against the enemies of King Aram's kingdom. Naaman was a brave soldier, but he had sores on his skin.

King Aram wrote a letter to the king of Israel. He asked the king to heal Naaman. The king of Israel read the letter and was mad. He said, "I am not God! I cannot heal people!"

Elisha heard about Naaman's problem. He sent a messenger to Naaman. The messenger told Naaman to come to Elisha's house. Elisha sent a man to the door to meet Naaman. The man said, "Elisha wants you to go to the Jordan River and wash yourself seven times. Your skin will be healed."

Naaman was angry. He wanted Elisha to come outside and pray for him. Naaman did not think that the Jordan River would make him well. He went away.

Naaman's friends said, "You should do what Elisha said. Wash yourself. Then, your skin will be healed."

Naaman went to the Jordan River. He washed himself seven times. The sores were gone!

Naaman told Elisha, "Now I know that the God of Israel is real. Here is a gift for you."

Elisha would not take the gift. He said, "I serve the Lord. You can be sure that He lives. Go in peace."

Say It! "'. . . Now I know that there is no God in all the world except in Israel.'" 2 Kings 5:15

Pray It! Lord, help me to follow You faithfully.

Explore It! Why was Naaman angry with Elisha? Tell about some good advice that a friend has given you.

Esther Saves Her People

What's missing?

Missing: Esther's crown

Esther Saves Her People

Esther 2:1–7, 2:17, 3:1–6, 4–5, 7:1–7

Mordecai was a Jewish man. He belonged to an Israelite family. He had a cousin named Esther. Mordecai took care of Esther after her parents died. When Esther grew up, she married the king. He put a crown on Esther's head and made her the queen.

The king had a helper named Haman. The king said that everyone must kneel in front of Haman. Mordecai would not kneel because he worshipped only God.

Haman planned to destroy Mordecai and the other Jewish people in the kingdom. Mordecai said to Esther, "Go to the king and beg for the safety of the Jewish people. We will pray."

Esther wanted to save the Jewish people. Esther was afraid to ask the king because he did not know that she was Jewish. Mordecai said, "Maybe God made you queen so that you could help your people."

Esther planned a big feast for Haman and the king. At the end of the dinner, the king asked, "Esther, what can I do for you? I will grant your wish."

Esther said, "My people and I will be destroyed. Please save us."

"Who would allow this?" the king asked.

"Haman," Esther answered. The king believed her and stopped the plan. Esther saved the Jewish people!

Say It! "Then Queen Esther answered, 'If I have found favor with you, O king, and if it pleases your majesty, grant me my life—this is my petition. And spare my people—this is my request.'" Esther 7:3

Pray It! Thank You, God, for having wonderful plans for us.

Explore It! Who did Haman want to destroy? How do you look out for your family members?

The King's Dream

What's missing?

Missing: statue

The King's Dream

Daniel 1:1–17, 2

Daniel and three of his friends were in the king's army. They followed God's rules. God gave an important gift to Daniel and his friends. God showed them the meanings of dreams.

The king was worried about a dream that he had. He sent for wise men and magicians. They could not explain his dream. The king was angry. He told Daniel to get rid of the wise men and magicians.

Daniel asked his friends to pray for God's help. God showed Daniel the meaning of the king's dream. Daniel said to the king, "God has told me your dream."

Daniel told the king, "I see a statue in your dream. It has a gold head and silver arms. The other parts are made of bronze, iron, and clay." Daniel told the king that the dream meant that God would give him great power. Three more kings would rule after the king. Then, God would make a new kingdom that would last forever.

The king said, "Your God is the greatest of all. He is the Lord of kings."

The king thanked Daniel and his friends. He asked them to help him rule the kingdom.

Say It! "The king said to Daniel, 'Surely your God is the God of gods and the Lord of kings.'" Daniel 2:47

Pray It! Thank You, God, for giving us a kingdom that will last forever.

Explore It! What gift did God give to Daniel and his friends? What is a gift that God has given you?

Saved from the Fire

Who's missing?

Missing: angel

Saved from the Fire

Daniel 3

The king was worried about a dream that he had. Daniel helped him understand the meaning of the dream. Then, the king asked Daniel and his friends to help him rule the kingdom.

The king built a statue like the one that he saw in his dream. He told the people to kneel and worship the statue every time they heard a flute, harp, horn, or other music. If people did not kneel, they would be thrown into a flaming furnace.

Daniel's friends, Shadrach, Meshach, and Abednego, would not kneel to the statue. They said, "We will worship only our God."

The king was angry. He asked, "Will your God save you from the fire?"

"We are not afraid," the men said. "If you throw us into the fire, God will save us."

The king told his servants to make the fire hotter. He told them to tie the men with ropes and throw them into the furnace. The servants obeyed the king.

The king looked in the furnace. He jumped to his feet and shouted, "You threw only three men into the fire! Why do I see four men? One looks like an angel. They are not tied up. They are walking around, and the fire is not burning them!" The king told the men to come out of the furnace.

Shadrach, Meshach, and Abednego came out with no burns on their bodies or clothing. They did not smell like smoke.

The king praised God for sending an angel to save the men from the fire. The king gave the men more power to help him rule the kingdom.

Say It!   ". . . They saw that the fire had not harmed their bodies, nor was a hair of their heads singed; their robes were not scorched, and there was no smell of fire on them." Daniel 3:27

Pray It!   Thank You, God, for working miracles.

Explore It!   How many people did the king see in the furnace? Tell about a time when God sent someone to help you.

Daniel in the Lions' Den

What should there be more of in this picture?

Missing: more lions

Daniel in the Lions' Den

Daniel 6

Daniel helped rule the kingdom. The king trusted Daniel. He wanted to put Daniel in charge of the whole kingdom.

Some of the king's men did not want Daniel to be so powerful. They planned to get rid of him. They said to the king, "You should make a new law. Tell the people that they must pray to you for 30 days. If they pray to any gods, they will be thrown into the lions' den." The king agreed.

The men went to Daniel's home. They saw him praying to God. When they told the king, he was sad. The king did not want to hurt Daniel, but the laws of the kingdom could not be changed.

The king's men took Daniel to the lions' den. The king said to Daniel, "You have always honored your God. I hope He will save you." The men put a large stone in front of the door. Daniel could not get out of the lions' den.

The king could not eat or sleep that night because he was worried about Daniel. Early the next morning, the king went to the lions' den. The stone was still in place. The king called, "Daniel, did your God save you?"

Daniel answered, "Yes, an angel closed the mouths of the lions. They have not hurt me."

The king was happy. He told his men to let Daniel out. The king wrote a letter to the people of every country and language in his kingdom. He wrote, "I order you to respect Daniel's God. He is the living God. His kingdom will not be destroyed, and He will rule forever."

Say It!   "'He rescues and he saves; he performs signs and wonders in the heavens and on the earth. He has rescued Daniel from the power of the lions.'" Daniel 6:27

Pray It!   Thank You for being the living God.

Explore It!   Why was Daniel thrown into the lions' den? Describe a time when you told someone about God.

Jonah and the Storm

What's missing?

Missing: stormy sky and high waves

Jonah and the Storm

Jonah 1:1–16

God wanted Jonah to talk to people who were doing bad things. He told Jonah to go to the city where the people lived. But, Jonah did not listen to God. Jonah ran away from God. He got on a ship that was sailing to another place.

God sent a strong wind across the sea. The sky became stormy. The sailors on the ship thought that their ship would break. They threw things overboard to make the ship lighter. They prayed to their gods for help.

Jonah did not help the men, and he did not pray to God. Jonah went below deck and fell asleep. The captain of the ship asked Jonah, "How can you sleep? Call on your God to save us from this terrible storm."

Jonah knew why God sent the storm. It was because Jonah disobeyed God. Jonah told the captain, "Throw me overboard, and the storm will stop." The men did not want to throw Jonah into the sea. They tried to row the ship back to land, but the storm got worse.

The men knew that they would drown. They prayed to Jonah's God for forgiveness. Then, they threw Jonah into the water.

The stormy sea was calm again. When the men saw what happened, they believed in the power of Jonah's God.

Say It!   "'Pick me up and throw me into the sea,' he replied, 'and it will become calm. I know that it is my fault that this great storm has come upon you.'" Jonah 1:12

Pray It!   Thank You, God, for calming storms.

Explore It!   Why did God send such a bad storm? Can you think of a time when you did not do what God would want? What happened?

Jonah and the Big Fish

What's missing?

Missing: big fish

Jonah and the Big Fish

Jonah 1–3

Jonah was on a ship. He was running away from God. A terrible storm came, and the ship was going to sink. Jonah told the sailors, "Throw me into the ocean, and the storm will stop." The sailors did what Jonah said, and the storm stopped.

Jonah sank to the bottom of the ocean. He almost drowned. God sent a large fish to swallow Jonah. Jonah was inside the fish for three days. Jonah prayed to God, "I know that You are the one who saves. I will do whatever You want me to do, Lord. I promise."

God told the fish to spit Jonah onto dry land. Jonah kept his promise to obey God. He went to the city. He told the people that they must change their ways and follow God. Jonah said, "If you do not obey God, He will destroy your city in 40 days."

The ruler of the city believed Jonah. He told the people to stop their evil ways. They listened to the ruler and prayed to God. God forgave the people and did not destroy their city.

Say It! "When God saw what they did and how they turned from their evil ways, he had compassion and did not bring upon them the destruction he had threatened." Jonah 3:10

Pray It! Help us, God, to change our bad habits.

Explore It! What did Jonah say would happen if the people did not stop their evil ways? Tell about a time when you gave someone a second chance.

Gabriel's Good News

Who's missing?

Missing: Gabriel

Gabriel's Good News

Luke 1:26–56

Mary lived in Nazareth. She planned to marry Joseph.

God sent an angel to visit Mary. The angel's name was Gabriel. Gabriel said, "The Lord is with you. He is very pleased with you."

Mary was worried. She did not understand why the angel came to her.

"Do not be afraid," Gabriel said. "You will have a son, and you should name him Jesus. He will be the Son of God. He will rule forever, and His kingdom will never end."

"How can this be?" Mary asked Gabriel.

The angel said, "The Holy Spirit will make this happen. Nothing is impossible with God."

"I serve God," Mary said. "Let this happen to me."

Mary hurried to visit her cousin Elizabeth. She knew that Elizabeth was going to have a baby too.

As soon as Elizabeth heard Mary, she was filled with the Holy Spirit. Elizabeth said, "You are blessed above all women. Your child is blessed too. You will be the mother of my Lord!"

Say It! "'I am the Lord's servant,' Mary answered. 'May it be to me as you have said.' Then the angel left her." Luke 1:38

Pray It! Lord, help me to always serve You.

Explore It! Who told Mary that she would have a son? What would you do if an angel appeared to you?

Jesus Is Born

Who's missing?

Missing: Baby Jesus

Jesus Is Born

Luke 2:1–21

The most powerful ruler of the land made a new law. He said that every man must go to the town where he was born to be counted.

Joseph was born in Bethlehem, so he and Mary went there to be counted. It was almost time for Mary to have her baby. Bethlehem was filled with people waiting to be counted. There was no place for Joseph and Mary to sleep.

Mary and Joseph found a place to stay. It was a place where animals slept. It had a manger to hold the animals' food. When the baby boy was born, Mary wrapped Him in cloths and placed Him in the empty manger.

Shepherds were watching their flocks in the fields near Bethlehem. An angel came to them, and they were scared. The angel said, "Do not be afraid! I have great news for you and for all people. The Savior of the world has been born! You can find Him lying in a manger in Bethlehem."

More angels appeared to the shepherds. They said, "Glory to God in the highest, and peace on earth."

When the angels left, the shepherds went to Bethlehem to see the baby. They found Him lying in a manger. The shepherds told people the great news. They praised God for everything that they heard and saw that night.

Say It! "and she gave birth to her firstborn, a son. She wrapped him in cloths and placed him in a manger, because there was no room for them in the inn." Luke 2:7

Pray It! Lord, we praise You for giving us Jesus.

Explore It! Where did Mary have her baby? Tell about a time when you had to change your plans because of a problem.

Wise Men Follow a Star

What's missing?

Missing: star of Bethlehem

Wise Men Follow a Star

Matthew 2:1–12

Jesus was born in Judea in the city of Bethlehem. Far away from Bethlehem, Wise Men watched the sky and studied the stars. They saw a special star. They followed it to a city near Bethlehem.

The Wise Men asked the people, "Where is the child who is the king of the Jews? We saw His star. We have come to worship Him."

Herod was the king of Judea. He heard that the Wise Men were looking for Jesus. King Herod did not want Jesus to be king. Herod said, "I want to speak to the Wise Men."

The Wise Men came to King Herod. He said to them, "Look for the child. When you find Him, tell me where He is. I want to worship Him too." But, King Herod was not telling the Wise Men the truth. He wanted to get rid of Jesus.

The Wise Men followed the star to Bethlehem. The star stopped over the house where Jesus was. The Wise Men saw the child with His mother, Mary. They bowed to Him and worshipped Him. They gave Him gifts of gold, incense, and myrrh.

Later, the Wise Men shared the same dream. The dream told them not to go back to King Herod. They did what the dream said. They did not tell King Herod where Jesus was. The Wise Men went home another way.

Say It! "On coming to the house, they saw the child with his mother Mary, and they bowed down and worshiped him. Then they opened their treasures and presented him with gifts of gold and of incense and of myrrh." Matthew 2:11

Pray It! Thank You, God, for leading us to Jesus.

Explore It! How did the Wise Men find Jesus? Describe a time when you followed God's lead.

Joseph's Dream

What's missing?

Missing: Mary and Joseph's belongings

Joseph's Dream

Matthew 2:13–23

Joseph had a dream. An angel told him to take Mary and Jesus to Egypt. The angel said, "The child is not safe in Israel. King Herod wants to kill Him. Stay in Egypt until I tell you to leave."

Joseph, Mary, and Jesus left that night. King Herod sent his men to Bethlehem. They looked for Jesus, but they could not find Him.

Joseph and his family stayed in Egypt until King Herod died. Joseph had another dream. An angel told him, "Get up! It is safe in Israel now. Take Jesus and Mary back."

Joseph woke his family. They packed their belongings and left Egypt. They traveled until they were near Bethlehem. Joseph learned that the new king was King Herod's son! Joseph was afraid that the new king would also want to hurt Jesus.

Joseph had another dream. The dream told Joseph to go to a safer place. Joseph, Mary, and Jesus went to live in Nazareth.

Say It!   ". . . an angel of the Lord appeared to Joseph in a dream. 'Get up,' he said. 'Take the child and his mother and escape to Egypt. Stay there until I tell you, for Herod is going to search for the child to kill him.'" Matthew 2:13

Pray It!   Father in heaven, thank You for keeping us safe.

Explore It! Where did Jesus' family escape to? Describe a time when you helped someone who did not feel safe.

Where Is Jesus?

Who's missing?

Missing: Jesus

Where Is Jesus?

Luke 2:41–52

Mary, Joseph, and twelve-year-old Jesus went to Jerusalem. They shared the Passover Feast with their family and friends. They celebrated the Passover Feast each year.

The Passover Feast ended, and the people were traveling home. Mary and Joseph were with a group going to Nazareth. They thought that Jesus was with the group.

At the end of the day, Mary and Joseph realized that Jesus was not with them. They looked among their friends and relatives. No one had seen Him. Mary and Joseph hurried back to Jerusalem to look for Jesus.

Three days later, they found Jesus. He was sitting in a garden outside of the temple. Jesus was listening to the teachers. He was asking questions. Jesus' answers surprised the teachers. They could not believe that a boy his age knew so much.

Mary said to Jesus, "We have been looking everywhere for You. We were worried!"

Jesus asked, "Why were you looking for Me? Didn't you know that I would be in My Father's house?"

Mary and Joseph did not understand what Jesus was saying to them. Jesus was telling them that the temple was God's house.

The family returned to Nazareth. Jesus grew stronger and wiser. God was pleased with His son, Jesus.

Say It!   "And the child grew and became strong; he was filled with wisdom, and the grace of God was upon him." Luke 2:40

Pray It!   Thank You, Lord, for blessing my family and me.

Explore It! Where did Mary and Joseph find Jesus? Tell about a time when someone thought that you were lost.

John the Baptist

What's missing?

Missing: hairy texture of tunic

John the Baptist

Luke 1:57–60, 3:2–16; Mark 1:4–8

Elizabeth and Zechariah had a baby boy. They named him John. When John grew up, he lived in the desert. He wore clothes made from camel hair. He ate wild honey and insects.

John heard God's Word in the desert. God had a special job for John. God wanted John to tell people that Jesus would be coming soon.

John traveled to many places around the Jordan River. He talked to people about sin and forgiveness. He told them to stop doing bad things. He said that God would forgive them for their mistakes. The people asked John, "What should we do?"

John gave the people rules to follow. He said, "Be happy with what you have. Share with others. Do not take things from others. Do not say bad things about people."

John baptized people in the river. He told the people to be ready because Jesus was coming soon. John said to the people, "I baptize you with water. Someone more powerful than me will come. He will baptize you with the Holy Spirit of God."

Say It!   "John answered them all, 'I baptize you with water. But one more powerful than I will come. . . . He will baptize you with the Holy Spirit and with fire.'" Luke 3:16

Pray It!   Help me, Lord, to be happy with what I have.

Explore It!   What rules did John give the people? What does it mean to be happy with what you have?

John Baptizes Jesus

What's missing?

Missing: dove

John Baptizes Jesus

John 1:19–34; Luke 3:21–22; Matthew 3:5–17

John the Baptist was at the Jordan River. He was preaching and baptizing people in the river. Some men asked John the Baptist, "Are you Jesus Christ? Are you the one who will save us?"

John told the men that he was not Jesus. John said, "Jesus is more powerful than I am. He will baptize you with the Holy Spirit."

Then, Jesus came to the river. John said to the people, "Look! Here is the man I have told you about. He will take away the sins of the world. He is the Son of God."

Jesus asked John to baptize Him. John did not think he was important enough to baptize Jesus. Jesus told John, "It is right for you to do this."

John baptized Jesus in the river. Jesus prayed, and heaven opened. A dove flew to Jesus and landed on Him. Then, a voice from heaven said to Jesus, "You are My Son, and I love You. I am pleased with You."

Say It! ". . . and the Holy Spirit descended on him in bodily form like a dove. And a voice came from heaven: 'You are my Son, whom I love; with you I am well pleased.'" Luke 3:22

Pray It! Thank You, God, for making baptism a new beginning for us.

Explore It! What did God say to Jesus after He was baptized? What makes God pleased with you?

The Devil Tries to Trick Jesus

What's missing?

Missing: bread in thought balloon

The Devil Tries to Trick Jesus

Luke 4:1–13; Mark 1:12–13

After Jesus was baptized, He left the Jordan River. God's Holy Spirit led Jesus to the desert. Wild animals were in the desert. Angels protected Jesus from the animals.

The devil tried to trick Jesus for 40 days. Jesus was hungry. He had not eaten for 40 days. The devil said to Jesus, "If You are the Son of God, turn these rocks into bread."

Jesus knew that the devil was trying to get Him to do the wrong thing. Jesus said to the devil, "Man does not live on bread alone."

The devil took Jesus to a high place. He showed Jesus every kingdom in the world. The devil said, "I will give the world to You if You will worship me."

Jesus told the devil, "God is the only One that I worship."

The devil led Jesus to Jerusalem. He told Jesus to stand on the highest point of the temple. The devil said, "Jump down from here. If You are the Son of God, the angels will save You."

Jesus did not jump. Jesus told the devil, "God has told us not to test His power."

The devil left. He could not trick Jesus. The devil planned to try again at another time.

Say It! "Jesus said to him, 'Away from me, Satan! For it is written: Worship the Lord your God, and serve him only.'" Matthew 4:10

Pray It! Thank You, God, for helping me say "no" to the devil.

Explore It! For how many days did the devil try to trick Jesus in the desert? Describe a time when you were tempted to do something that God wouldn't want you to do.

Peter Follows Jesus

What's missing?

Missing: fish

Peter Follows Jesus

Luke 5:1–11; Matthew 4:18–20

Jesus stood near the Sea of Galilee. He was teaching people about God. Jesus saw two fishing boats on the shore. The fishermen were washing their nets.

Jesus went onto Peter's boat. Jesus asked Peter to row a short distance from the shore. Jesus sat on the boat and talked to the people on the shore. When He finished talking, Jesus told Peter, "Row the boat into deeper water. Let down the nets."

Peter said, "We worked hard all night. We did not catch any fish. But, because You say so, I will let down the nets."

Peter dropped the nets into the water. The nets filled with fish. There were so many fish that the nets started to break. The fishermen on the other boat came to help. They filled the boats with fish. Both boats began to sink.

Peter and his friends were amazed. Jesus said to them, "From now on, you will catch people, not fish."

The men pulled their boats to shore. They knew that Jesus was giving them a new job. Jesus wanted them to teach people about God.

Peter and his friends left everything and followed Jesus. They were Jesus' first disciples.

Say It!   ". . . Then Jesus said to Simon, 'Don't be afraid; from now on you will catch men.' So they pulled their boats up on shore, left everything and followed him." Luke 5:10–11

Pray It!   Thank You, God, for allowing me to be a fisher for You.

Explore It! What job did Peter have before he was a disciple for Jesus? What have you told someone about Jesus?

Jesus Turns Water into Wine

What's missing?

Missing: wine pouring into cup

Jesus Turns Water into Wine

John 2:1–11

Jesus chose a few men to be His disciples. They helped Jesus teach people about God.

Jesus, His mother Mary, and His disciples went to a wedding. There was a party after the wedding. At the party, Mary told Jesus, "There is no more wine." Mary knew that Jesus could help.

Mary told the servants, "Do what Jesus tells you."

Jesus saw six stone jars. Each jar could hold 20 to 30 gallons of water. Jesus told the servants, "Fill those jars with water."

The servants filled each jar. Jesus said, "Pour some into a cup. Give it to the man in charge of the dinner." The servants did what Jesus told them.

The man drank from the cup. It was wine! The servants knew that Jesus had turned the water into wine.

This was Jesus' first miracle. When the disciples saw this miracle, their faith in Jesus grew.

Say It! "and the master of the banquet tasted the water that had been turned into wine. He did not realize where it had come from, though the servants who had drawn the water knew." John 2:9

Pray It! Help me, Jesus, to always do what You tell me.

Explore It! Who told Jesus that the people needed more wine? Have you ever seen a miracle? Tell about it.

A Hole in the Roof

What's missing?

Missing: man lying on mat

A Hole in the Roof

Mark 2:1–12

Jesus was preaching in a crowded place. There was no room to sit or stand. Some people stood outside to listen to Jesus.

Four men came to ask Jesus to heal their friend. Their friend could not walk, so they carried him on a mat. They could not fit through the door because there were so many people.

The men climbed to the roof. They made a hole in the roof. They lowered their friend through the roof.

Jesus saw the man on the mat. He said to the man, "Son, your sins are forgiven."

Some teachers of the law heard what Jesus said. They thought, "Jesus cannot forgive sins. He is not God."

Jesus knew what the teachers were thinking. Jesus told the teachers, "The Son of Man has the power to forgive sins."

Jesus said to the man on the mat, "Get up. Take your mat and go home."

Everyone was amazed to see the man stand up and walk. They praised God and said, "We have never seen anything like this!"

Say It! "He got up, took his mat and walked out in full view of them all. This amazed everyone and they praised God, saying, 'We have never seen anything like this.'" Mark 2:12

Pray It! Lord, we give You thanks for forgiving our sins.

Explore It! What did the men do when they could not fit their friend through the door? Tell about a time that a friend helped you when you couldn't do something.

The Story of the Farmer

What's missing?

Missing: seeds in each area

The Story of the Farmer

Mark 4:1–20

A large crowd gathered by a lake. Jesus got into a boat at the edge of the water. He sat on the boat and told the people a story.

Jesus said, "A farmer went to plant his seeds. He spread the seeds on the ground. Some seeds fell on a path. Birds came and ate every seed on the path. Some seeds fell on rocky places. The plants began to grow, but they did not have roots. The plants died.

"Other seeds fell into thorny plants. The thorny plants filled the ground. There was no room for the seeds to grow.

"Some seeds fell on good soil. They grew into healthy plants. The farmer gathered 100 times more grain than he planted."

Jesus' 12 disciples listened to the story too. They wondered why Jesus told a story about a farmer. No one understood what Jesus really meant.

Jesus told the disciples, "The farmer spreads his seeds like God spreads His Word. Some people hear God's Word, but the devil comes to them. He takes away God's Word like the birds took away the seeds."

Then Jesus said, "Some people hear God's Word with joy, but they lose their faith when trouble comes. Other people lose their faith when they want things that they cannot have. Their faith dies like the seeds on the rocks and thorns.

"People who keep their faith watch it grow. It will grow like the seeds on good soil."

Say It! "When he was alone, the Twelve and the others around him asked him about the parables. He told them, 'The secret of the kingdom of God has been given to you. But to those on the outside everything is said in parables.'" Mark 4:10–11

Pray It! God, help my faith grow.

Explore It! What happens to some people when they want things that they cannot have? Describe a time when you wanted something that you could not have.

Jesus Heals a Woman

What's missing?

Missing: woman's arm with hand touching Jesus' robe

Jesus Heals a Woman

Mark 5:22–34

A large crowd was following Jesus. He was going to a man's house. Along the way, a woman joined the group. She had heard that Jesus could heal people.

The woman had been sick for 12 years. Every year, she got worse. She wanted Jesus to heal her. She said, "If I just touch His clothes, I will be healed."

The woman moved through the crowd until she got close to Jesus. She touched His clothes. Instantly, she felt better. Her body was healed.

Jesus felt some of His power go out of Him when the woman touched Him. Jesus asked, "Who touched my clothes?"

Many people were crowding against Jesus. Jesus' disciples were near Him. They were surprised that Jesus could feel such a soft touch in the large crowd.

The woman was afraid to tell Jesus that she touched His clothes. She kneeled in front of Jesus and told Him the truth.

Jesus said, "Daughter, go in peace. You are free from your sickness. You have been healed because you had faith."

Say It! "He said to her, 'Daughter, your faith has healed you. Go in peace and be freed from your suffering.'" Mark 5:34

Pray It! Thank You, God, for Your healing power.

Explore It! How did Jesus know that someone touched His clothes? Tell about a time when you felt better after you told the truth.

Jesus Teaches the Lord's Prayer

What's missing?

Missing: mountains and more people

Jesus Teaches the Lord's Prayer

Matthew 4:23–25, 5:1–2, 6:5–15

People followed Jesus everywhere that He went. They heard that Jesus could heal sick people. One crowd was so large that Jesus had to go onto the side of a mountain to preach. His disciples joined Him.

Jesus explained how to pray. He told the people, "When you pray, go into your room, close the door, and pray to your Father, who can't be seen. Your Father sees what is done in private, and He will reward you."

Jesus said that we should forgive people who sin against us. He said that if we forgive others, then God will forgive us when we make mistakes.

Jesus said, "This is how you should pray:

"'Our Father in heaven, hallowed be Your name, Your kingdom come, Your will be done on earth as it is in heaven. Give us today our daily bread. Forgive us our debts, as we also have forgiven our debtors. And lead us not into temptation, but deliver us from the evil one.'"

Say It! "'For if you forgive men when they sin against you, your heavenly Father will also forgive you. But if you do not forgive men their sins, your Father will not forgive your sins.'" Matthew 6:14–15

Pray It! Thank You, Jesus, for teaching us how to pray.

Explore It! What should we do about a person who sins against us? Do you know how to pray the Lord's Prayer?

Jesus Calms a Storm

What's missing?

Missing: stormy sky and high waves

Jesus Calms a Storm

8:23–27

One night, Jesus and His disciples got into a boat on a lake. When they left the shore, the night was peaceful and calm. Jesus went to sleep.

Suddenly, a terrible storm came. The calm lake became rough. The wind began to roar. Waves crashed over the sides of the boat. Jesus continued to sleep.

The disciples woke Jesus. They begged Him, "Please save us, or we will drown!"

Jesus said, "Your faith is so small. Why are you afraid?"

Jesus got up. He ordered the wind and the waves to stop. They became calm. The storm ended.

The disciples were amazed by Jesus' great power. They asked, "What kind of man is this? Even the winds and the waves obey Him!"

Say It!   "He replied, 'You of little faith, why are you so afraid?' Then he got up and rebuked the winds and the waves, and it was completely calm." Matthew 8:26

Pray It!   Father, thank You for helping us not to be afraid.

Explore It!   What was Jesus doing when the storm started? What storms or problems in your life can Jesus take care of?

Dinner for 5,000

What's missing?

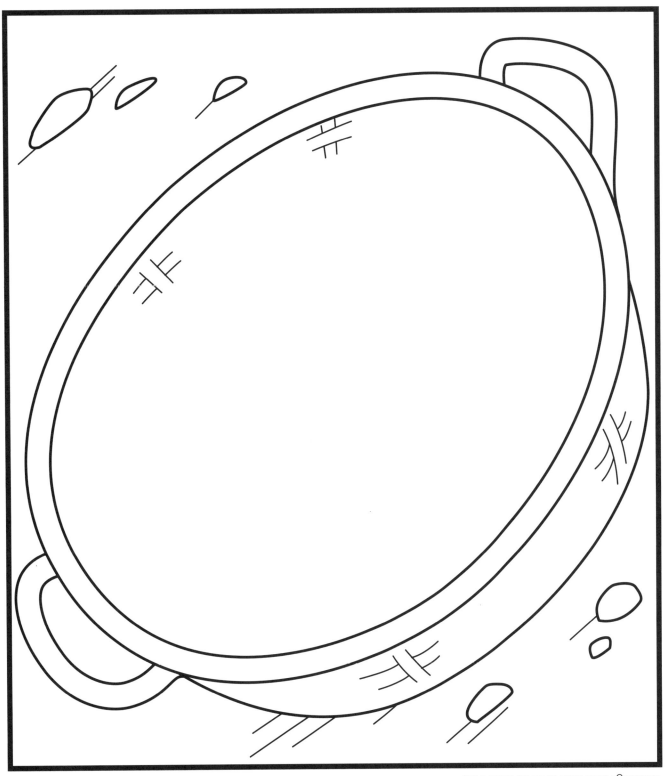

Missing: fish and loaves of bread

Dinner for 5,000

Mark 6:30–44; John 6:9; Matthew 14:21

Jesus and His disciples had been talking to a large crowd of people for many hours. It was late in the afternoon, and the people were hungry. They had not eaten all day.

The disciples did not have food to give the people. The disciples asked Jesus to tell the people to go home. "There is no food here," they told Him. "The people are very hungry. Please send them away so that they can eat."

Jesus answered, "They do not need to leave. Give them something to eat."

The disciples did not have enough money to buy food for 5,000 men. Jesus asked His disciples, "How much food is here? Go and see."

Andrew was a disciple. He told Jesus, "Here is a boy with five small loaves of bread and two small fish. That will not be enough for 5,000 men."

Jesus told His disciples to ask the people to sit. Then, Jesus looked to heaven and gave thanks. He broke the five loaves and divided the two fish. He told the disciples to give the bread and the fish to the people.

Women, children, and 5,000 men ate as much as they wanted. Jesus told the disciples to collect the leftovers. The disciples returned to Jesus with 12 baskets filled with bread and fish. It was a miracle!

Say It! "They all ate and were satisfied, and the disciples picked up twelve basketfuls of broken pieces of bread and fish. The number of the men who had eaten was five thousand." Mark 6:42–44

Pray It! Lord, thank You for always supplying enough.

Explore It! How many men were fed by the little boy's food? Give an example of how God provides what you need, even if you don't get what you want.

Jesus Walks on Water

Who's missing?

Missing: Jesus walking on water

Jesus Walks on Water

Matthew 14:22–33

Jesus told the disciples to get into the boat and go to the other side of the lake. Jesus stayed behind. He went on a mountainside to pray until late at night.

The disciples were in the boat far across the lake. They saw someone coming to the boat. He was walking on the water! The disciples were afraid. They cried, "It is a ghost!"

Jesus told them who He was. He told them not to be afraid.

Peter said, "Lord, if it is You, tell me to come to You on the water."

Jesus told Peter to come. Peter got out of the boat and began to walk on the water.

The wind started to blow, and Peter was afraid. He began to sink. He called to Jesus, "Lord, save me!"

Jesus told Peter, "You do not have much faith. Why did you doubt Me?"

Then, Jesus took Peter's hand. They climbed into the boat. The wind stopped blowing.

The disciples on the boat saw what happened. They said, "You are truly the Son of God."

Say It! "Immediately Jesus reached out his hand and caught him. 'You of little faith,' He said, 'why did you doubt?'" Matthew 14:31

Pray It! Thank You, God, for saving me when I'm in trouble.

Explore It! Why did Peter begin to sink? Describe a time when you felt scared, then realized you shouldn't be afraid.

A Fish with Money in Its Mouth

What's missing?

Missing: coin

A Fish with Money in Its Mouth

Matthew 17:24–27

Every year, the tax collectors visited the people. Everyone had to give money to the collectors for the temple tax.

The tax collectors came to Peter. They asked him, "Doesn't your friend Jesus pay the temple tax?"

Peter answered, "Yes, He does." Peter went into the house where Jesus was. Peter did not need to tell Jesus about the tax collectors' question. Jesus already knew.

Jesus said that He should not have to pay any taxes because His Father was the Lord over all kings. But, Jesus did not want to make the tax collectors angry. He wanted to obey the king's laws. Jesus had a plan to get the money for the tax.

Jesus told Peter to go to the lake. He told Peter to put his fishing line into the water. Jesus said, "Take the first fish that you catch. Open its mouth. You will find a coin. Take it and give it to the tax collector. It is enough money to pay for My tax and yours."

Say It! "'. . . go to the lake, and throw out your line. Take the first fish you catch; open its mouth and you will find a four–drachma coin. Take it and give it to them for my tax and yours.'" Matthew 17:27

Pray It! We praise You, Lord, for hidden blessings.

Explore It! Why did Jesus agree to pay the taxes? Tell about a time when you found something you needed in a strange place.

The Lost Sheep

What should there be more of in this picture?

Missing: more sheep

The Lost Sheep

Luke 15:1–7

A large crowd gathered around Jesus. Tax collectors and teachers of the law were in the crowd. They did not like to see Jesus being kind to the sinners in the crowd. They did not want to be near people who were sinners. They said, "This man welcomes sinners and eats with them."

Jesus wanted the people to know that God loves everyone. God is happy when a person stops sinning and comes back to God. Jesus told the people a story to help them understand.

Jesus said, "A man has 100 sheep and loses one. Won't he leave the 99 and look for the lost sheep? When he finds it, he will be happy. He will put the sheep on his shoulders and go home. The man will invite his friends and neighbors to celebrate with him. He will tell them, 'I have found my lost sheep. I want to share my happiness with you.'"

Then, Jesus told the crowd that God feels the same way. God is happy in heaven when a sinner finds the way back to God.

Say It! "I tell you that in the same way there will be more rejoicing in heaven over one sinner who repents than over ninety-nine righteous persons who do not need to repent.'" Luke 15:7

Pray It! Lord, I am blessed that You never give up on me!

Explore It! Why did the man want his neighbors to celebrate with him? Have you ever found something that you lost, and you wanted to celebrate? Describe what happened.

The Good Samaritan

What's missing?

Missing: liquid pouring on man's injuries

The Good Samaritan
Luke 10:25–37

Jesus was talking to a large group of people. A man asked Jesus, "What must I do to live forever in heaven?"

Jesus said, "What does the law say?"

The man answered, "Love God with all your heart and with all your soul. Love Him with all your strength and with all your mind. Love your neighbor as much as you love yourself."

Jesus said, "Do this and you will live."

Then, the man asked Jesus, "Who is my neighbor?" Jesus wanted the man to know that everyone is your neighbor. He told this story to help the man understand.

Jesus said, "A Jewish man was walking from Jerusalem to Jericho. Robbers attacked him. They took everything that he had. They left him lying near the road.

"A priest walked by and saw the man. He crossed to the other side of the road. The priest did not stop to help the man. Another man walked by and did the same thing. He also crossed to the other side of the road.

"The next man who walked by was a Samaritan. He lived in a country near Israel. The Jewish people did not like Samaritans. But, the Samaritan stopped to help anyway. He treated the hurt man like a neighbor. He cleaned the man's cuts with wine and oil. He put the man on a donkey and took him to town. The Samaritan paid someone to take care of the man."

When Jesus finished this story, He asked, "Which of these three men was a good neighbor to the hurt man?"

The man in the crowd answered, "The one who stopped to help him."

Jesus said, "You should be a good neighbor to others too."

Say It! "'Which of these three . . . was a neighbor to the man . . . ?' The expert in the law replied, 'The one who had mercy on him.' Jesus told him, 'Go and do likewise.'" Luke 10:36–37

Pray It! Thank You, God, for loving all people the same.

Explore It! Who stayed and helped the man? What do you do to show love to people who are different from you?

Jesus Visits Mary and Martha

What's missing?

Missing: broom or other cleaning items

Jesus Visits Mary and Martha

Luke 10:38–42

Jesus and His disciples traveled to many towns. They slept at people's houses along the way.

In one town, there were sisters named Martha and Mary. Martha invited Jesus to come to their home.

Jesus went into the house. He sat down, and Mary sat on the floor next to Jesus' feet. She wanted to hear every word that Jesus said.

Martha did not sit and listen to Jesus. She was working to make the house ready for Jesus.

Mary did not get up to help her sister. Martha went to Jesus and said, "Don't You care that I do all of this work by myself? Tell Mary to help me."

Jesus said, "Martha, Martha. You should not worry about so many things. Mary has chosen the right thing to do. She has chosen to be with Me. I will not take that away from her."

Say It! "'Martha, Martha,' the Lord answered. 'You are worried and upset about many things, but only one thing is needed. Mary has chosen what is better, and it will not be taken away from her.'" Luke 10:41–42

Pray It! Father, help me to always put You first in my life.

Explore It! Why was Jesus at Mary and Martha's house? If Jesus were coming to your house for dinner, what would you do to get ready?

Jesus Heals a Blind Man

What's missing?

Missing: mud in Jesus' hand

Jesus Heals a Blind Man

John 9:1–11

As Jesus and His disciples walked, they saw a man. He had been blind since he was born. The disciples asked Jesus why the man was blind. They wanted to know if it was because he or his parents sinned.

Jesus said, "No, this happened so that God can show His work. We must do the work of the one who sent Me."

Jesus spit on the ground and made mud. He put the mud on the man's eyes. Jesus told the man to go to the water and wash his eyes.

The man did what Jesus said. He could see again! He went home and saw his neighbors. They asked, "Is this the same man who used to sit and beg?"

He said, "I am the same man. Jesus made some mud and put it on my eyes. He told me to go to the water and wash my eyes. So, I went and washed. Then, I could see."

Say It!   "'. . . this happened so that the work of God might be displayed in his life.'" John 9:3

Pray It!   Jesus, thank You for working in my life.

Explore It! Why was the man blind? Describe a time when God helped you turn a bad thing into a good thing.

The Good Shepherd

What's missing?

Missing: wolf

The Good Shepherd

John 9:24–38, 10:1–18

Some people did not like what Jesus taught. They did not believe that Jesus was the Son of God. Jesus wanted them to understand why God sent Him to earth. Jesus wanted them to know that He came to help people.

Jesus told the people a story to help them understand. He said, "A shepherd calls his sheep by name. The sheep will follow their shepherd because they know his voice. I am like the gate for the sheep. I keep out anyone who comes to hurt the sheep. I am the gate. Whoever enters through Me will be saved. I have come to give people a full life."

The people listened to the story, but they did not understand. Jesus told another story. He said, "If a wolf attacks the sheep, the shepherd will protect them. Another worker would run away from the wolf, but a good shepherd will risk his life for his sheep. I am the Good Shepherd, and the people are My sheep."

Jesus was saying that He wants to protect all people because He loves them. He promises to keep everyone who believes in Him safe.

Some of the people did not believe Jesus, but others put their faith in His words.

Say It! "'I am the Good Shepherd. The Good Shepherd lays down his life for the sheep.'" John 10:11

Pray It! Lord, I thank You for being a Good Shepherd to me.

Explore It! Why would another worker run away from the wolf? How is Jesus a Good Shepherd to you?

The Lost Son Comes Home

What should there be more of in this picture?

Missing: more pigs

The Lost Son Comes Home

Luke 15:10–32

Jesus wanted people to know that God is happy when someone comes back to Him. Jesus told this story to help the people understand.

Jesus said, "A man had two sons. The younger son asked for his half of his father's land. The man gave each son half of everything that he owned.

"The young son moved far away. He spent his money on foolish things. When he had no money left, he got a job feeding pigs. The young son was hungry, but no one gave him food. The young son decided to go back home. He wanted his father to forgive him.

"The father saw his young son and ran to him. He put his arms around his son and kissed him.

"The young son said, 'Father, I have sinned against heaven and you.' His father was not angry. He was so happy that he had a party for his son.

"The older son was working in the fields. He heard music and dancing. A servant told him, 'Your brother has come home. He is safe. Your father is having a party.'

"The older son was angry. He told his father, 'For many years I have worked hard for you. I have always obeyed you. My brother left home and wasted your money. Why are you having a party for him?'

"His father said, 'You are always with me. Everything I have is yours. But, your brother was lost. I thought that he was dead. Now he is found.'"

Say It!   "'My son,' the father said, 'you are always with me, and everything I have is yours. But we had to celebrate and be glad, because this brother of yours was dead and is alive again; he was lost and is found.'" Luke 15:31–32

Pray It!   Father in heaven, let me always be thankful when someone comes back to You.

Explore It! Why was the older brother angry when his brother came home? Tell about a time when someone did not notice your hard work.

Jesus Sees Zacchaeus

Who's missing?

Missing: Zacchaeus

Jesus Sees Zacchaeus

Luke 19:1–10

People paid money to tax collectors every year. The tax collectors gave the money to the city.

Some people thought that tax collectors were sinners. Some tax collectors collected money for the city, but they kept some for themselves.

Zacchaeus was a tax collector. He was rich. Jesus was passing through Zacchaeus's city. A large crowd gathered to see Jesus.

Zacchaeus ran ahead of the crowd. He wanted to see Jesus too. Zacchaeus was a short man. So, he climbed a tree to help him see Jesus better.

Jesus reached the place where Zacchaeus was. He looked up at Zacchaeus in the tree. Jesus said, "Zacchaeus, come down. I will stay at your house today."

The crowd was surprised that Jesus wanted to go to a sinner's house. Zacchaeus was happy to have Jesus as his guest.

Zacchaeus told Jesus, "I will give half of everything that I have to the poor. If I have taken people's money, I will pay them back four times." Jesus told Zacchaeus that God had forgiven him for the bad things that he had done.

Say It! "Jesus said to him, 'Today salvation has come to this house, because this man, too, is a son of Abraham. For the Son of Man came to seek and to save what was lost.'" Luke 19:9–10

Pray It! Thank You, God, for giving us a new life like you gave Zacchaeus.

Explore It! Why didn't people like Zacchaeus? Have you forgiven someone lately? How did it make you feel?

Washing Feet

What's missing?

Missing: water pouring from pitcher

Washing Feet

John 13:1–17

Jesus knew that soon He would leave earth. It was almost time for Jesus to go to His Father in heaven.

Jesus was eating dinner with His disciples. When they finished their meal, Jesus got up. He wrapped a towel around His waist. He poured water into a large bowl. Jesus wanted to show the disciples that He loved them.

Peter asked, "Lord, are You about to wash my feet?" He did not think that the Son of God should wash feet.

Jesus said, "Unless I wash you, you cannot share life with Me." Jesus wanted Peter to know that people should do kind things for each other.

Then, Jesus washed His disciples' feet. He used the towel to dry them.

When Jesus finished, He asked, "Do you understand what I have done for you? I am your Lord and your teacher, and I have washed your feet. I have given you an example. You should do for others what I have done for you."

Jesus was showing His disciples that one person is not more important than another. Everyone is important. Jesus said, "Now that you know these things, you will be blessed if you do them."

Say It! "I have set you an example that you should do as I have done for you. I tell you the truth, no servant is greater than his master, nor is a messenger greater than the one who sent him.'" John 13:15–16

Pray It! Lord, please help me remember that every person is important.

Explore It! Why did Jesus wash the disciples' feet? What can you do for your family to show them that they are important?

The Vine and the Branches

What's missing?

Missing: fruit on healthy branch

The Vine and the Branches

John 14:1–14, 15:5–12

The disciples knew that Jesus would leave them soon. Jesus said, "Do not be sad. Trust in God. Trust in Me too."

Jesus told the disciples that someday they would join Him in heaven. The disciples said that they did not know how to get to heaven.

Jesus said, "I am the way and the truth and the life. I am the only way to the Father." Jesus was telling the disciples that if they followed His ways, they would go to heaven.

Jesus gave the disciples an important job to do after He was gone. He told them to keep teaching people about God. He told them a story to help them understand.

Jesus said that God is like a gardener. A gardener wants his plants to grow fruit. Fruit grows on branches that are attached to the vine. If a branch is cut from the vine, it will dry up and die. Fruit cannot grow if the branch dies.

Jesus said, "I am the vine, and you are the branches." Jesus was saying that the disciples could do many good things on earth with His help. But, they must remember to keep Jesus close to them like the branches on a vine.

Jesus promised to help the disciples, even after He went to heaven. Jesus said, "Here is My command. Love each other, just like I have loved you."

Say It! "'This is my command. Love each other.'" John 15:17

Pray It! God, help me love others just like You love me.

Explore It! What happens to the fruit when a branch is cut from the vine? What will happen if we keep Jesus close to us every day?

A Donkey for a King

What's missing?

Missing: coats and branches

A Donkey for a King

Mark 11:1–11

Jesus and the disciples were traveling to Jerusalem. Jesus told His disciples to go ahead of Him to the next village. He said that they would see a young donkey that had never been ridden. He told the disciples to untie the donkey and bring it to Him.

The disciples found the donkey and untied it. Some people asked, "Why are you doing that?" The disciples told the people that Jesus wanted the donkey. The people let the disciples take the donkey.

The disciples gave the donkey to Jesus. They spread their coats on the donkey's back. Jesus rode the donkey, and they continued their trip.

The people of Jerusalem were happy to see Jesus coming. Some people spread their coats on the road. Others cut branches and laid them on the road. The people were treating Jesus like a king.

Many people walked in front of Jesus or followed behind Him. They shouted, "Blessed is He who comes in the name of the Lord!"

Say It! "Those who went ahead and those who followed shouted, 'Hosanna! Blessed is he who comes in the name of the Lord!'" Mark 11:9

Pray It! I give You thanks, God, for being a great king!

Explore It! What did people lay on the ground in front of Jesus? What can you do to treat Jesus like a king?

The Last Supper

What's missing?

Missing: bread and wine

The Last Supper

Matthew 26:1–2, 26:14–30; Luke 22:7–20

Priests and teachers of the law did not like Jesus. They wanted to get rid of Him. Jesus told His disciples, "After the Passover Feast, men will take Me away. I will be crucified."

A disciple named Judas went to the priests. The priests told Judas, "We will pay you if you give Jesus to us." Judas said that he would do it.

Two days later, Jesus ate the Passover meal with the disciples. Jesus said, "One of you will turn against Me."

Each disciple said sadly, "I am sure I will not turn against You."

Judas said, "Surely not me."

Jesus told him, "Yes, it is you."

While they were eating, Jesus picked up a piece of bread. He gave thanks and broke the bread. Jesus gave it to the disciples. He said, "Take this and eat it. This is My body. I am giving it for you." Jesus meant that He would take away everyone's sins when He died.

Then, He took a cup, gave thanks, and shared it with the disciples. Jesus said, "Drink from it, all of you. This is My blood of the new covenant. It will be poured out so that sins will be forgiven. Do this and remember Me."

Jesus wanted the disciples to know that He loved them. He would always be with them, even when He was in heaven.

Say It! "And he took bread, gave thanks and broke it, and gave it to them, saying, 'This is my body given for you; do this in remembrance of me.'" Luke 22:19

Pray It! Thank You, Jesus, for giving Your life for us.

Explore It! What did Jesus use to remind us of His body and His blood? Tell about a time when you helped someone feel better by telling them how much Jesus loves him.

Jesus Is Crucified

What's missing?

Missing: crown of thorns

Jesus Is Crucified

Luke 22:39–54, 23:1–46; Matthew 27:29

After the Last Supper, Jesus and His disciples went outside to pray. Jesus walked a short distance from them. He kneeled and prayed. When He went back to the disciples, they were asleep. While Jesus was waking them, a crowd came, and they took Him to their ruler, Pontius Pilate.

"Are you the king of the Jews?" Pilate asked Jesus.

"Yes, I am," Jesus said.

Pilate told the crowd that Jesus did nothing wrong. Pilate sent Jesus to another ruler named King Herod. King Herod also said that Jesus did nothing wrong.

King Herod and his soldiers made fun of Jesus. They dressed Him in a fancy robe. They put a crown of thorns on Jesus' head. Then, they sent Him back to Pilate.

Pilate's soldiers laughed at Him. They said, "Hail, king of the Jews!"

Pilate talked to the crowd. Pilate said, "Herod and I do not think that this man should die. I will punish Him. Then, I will let Him go."

The crowd wanted Jesus to die. They yelled, "Crucify Him! Crucify Him!" Pilate did what the crowd wanted. He gave the order to crucify Jesus.

People watched Jesus die. They laughed at Him and said, "He saved others. Let Him save Himself if He is the Christ, the Chosen One."

Jesus prayed, "Father, forgive them. They do not know what they are doing."

The sun stopped shining. Jesus called out to God, "Father, I put My spirit into Your hands." Jesus took His last breath.

Say It! "Jesus said, 'Father, forgive them, for they do not know what they are doing.'" Luke 23:34

Pray It! Thank You, Jesus, for taking away our sins.

Explore It! Why did Pilate give the order to have Jesus crucified? What can you tell a person who says something that hurts your feelings?

Jesus Is Not in the Tomb

What's missing?

Missing: pile of cloths

Jesus Is Not in the Tomb

John 19:40–42, 20:1–23; Luke 23:53, 24:36–49

After Jesus died, two men wrapped His body in pieces of cloth. They laid Him in a tomb that was cut into a rock.

Three days later, Mary Magdalene went to the tomb. The stone was moved from the opening. Mary ran to the disciples. She said, "They have taken Jesus. I don't know where they put Him."

Two disciples ran to the tomb. They saw the pieces of cloth, but Jesus was not there. The disciples did not understand that Jesus had risen from the dead. They went home.

Mary stayed outside the tomb and cried. She looked into the tomb and saw two angels dressed in white. They sat where Jesus had been.

The angels asked, "Why are you crying?"

Mary said, "They have taken my Lord away." Mary turned around. She saw a man standing near her. She did not know that the man was Jesus. He asked her, "Who are you looking for?"

Mary looked at Him again. She said, "Teacher!" because she knew he was Jesus.

Jesus said, "Go to the disciples. Tell them that I am returning to God."

Mary went to the disciples. She told them, "I have seen the Lord!"

Later that night, Jesus appeared to the disciples in a locked room. He said, "Peace be with you. The Father has sent Me. So now, I am sending you."

Jesus was telling the disciples to teach about God. Jesus breathed the Holy Spirit on the disciples. He said, "Now you have received the Holy Spirit. You can forgive people, and their sins will be taken away."

Say It! "Jesus said, 'Do not hold on to me, for I have not yet returned to the Father. Go instead to my brothers and tell them I am returning to my Father and your Father, to my God and your God.'" John 20:17

Pray It! Thank You, God, for giving us the Holy Spirit.

Explore It! Who did Mary see when she looked in the tomb? What has Jesus asked us to do?

Doubting Thomas

What's missing?

Missing: marks on Jesus' hands

Doubting Thomas

John 20:24–29

A few nights after Jesus died, the disciples gathered in a locked room. Jesus appeared in front of them. Thomas was not with the other disciples that night. Later, they told Thomas, "We have seen the Lord!"

Thomas thought that Jesus was still dead. Thomas told the other disciples, "I will not believe it until I see the marks on Jesus' hands where He was crucified. Then, I will believe you."

The next week, Jesus appeared in the locked room again. This time, all of the disciples were there. Jesus said, "Peace be with you."

Then, Jesus showed Thomas the marks on His hands. He told Thomas to stop doubting and start believing.

Thomas looked at the marks on Jesus' hands. Thomas said to Jesus, "My Lord and my God!"

Jesus said, "You believe that I am alive because you have seen Me. Blessed are the people who believe without seeing Me."

Say It! "Then Jesus told him, 'Because you have seen me, you have believed; blessed are those who have not seen and yet have believed.'" John 20:29

Pray It! I thank You, Jesus, for being a real part of my life.

Explore It! Why didn't Thomas believe that Jesus was alive? If Jesus appeared to you today, what would you say to Him?

Breakfast with Jesus

What's missing?

Missing: fish and bread

Breakfast with Jesus

John 21:1–14

Many days after Jesus died, Peter said, "I am going out on the boat to fish." Some of the other disciples went with him. They fished all night, but they did not catch any fish.

The next morning, they saw a man standing on the shore. They could not tell that the man was Jesus. He asked them, "Friends, do you have any fish?"

They said, "No."

The man told them to throw the net on the right side of the boat. He told them that they would catch fish there.

The disciples did what the man said. They caught so many fish that they could not lift the net.

One disciple looked at the man on the shore again. He said, "It is the Lord!" The disciple jumped into the water, and the others followed in the boat.

The disciples dragged the net to the shore. It had 153 large fish in it. When the disciples reached the shore, they saw fish and bread cooking on a fire. Jesus said to them, "Come and have breakfast."

Jesus shared the bread and fish with the disciples. This was the third time that Jesus appeared to the disciples after He died.

Say It!   "Jesus came, took the bread and gave it to them, and did the same with the fish. This was now the third time Jesus appeared to his disciples after he was raised from the dead." John 21:13–14

Pray It!   Lord Jesus, I am blessed that You want to spend time with me.

Explore It!   What happened when Jesus told the disciples to throw the nets on the right side? Where would you like to have breakfast with Jesus?

Peter's Second Chance

What's missing?

Missing: rooster

Peter's Second Chance

Matthew 26:34–35, 26:69–75; John 21:15–17

A few days before Jesus died, He told Peter, "The rooster will crow. Before it does, you will say three times that you do not know Me."

Peter thought that Jesus was wrong. He told Jesus, "I will never say that I do not know You."

Peter watched as men came to take Jesus away. People asked Peter if he knew Jesus. Peter said three times, "I do not know Him."

The third time Peter spoke, a rooster crowed. Peter cried. He was sad because he lied. It happened like Jesus said that it would.

Jesus visited the disciples after He died. He asked Peter, "Do you really love Me?"

Peter said, "Yes, Lord. You know that I love You."

Jesus said, "Feed My lambs."

Jesus asked Peter again, "Do you really love Me?"

Peter said, "Yes, Lord. You know that I love You."

Jesus said, "Take care of My sheep."

Jesus asked the same question again. Peter said, "Lord, You know all things. You know that I love You."

Jesus told Peter, "Feed My sheep."

Peter knew that Jesus was giving him a special job. Jesus wanted Peter to take care of the people who believed in Jesus.

Say It! "'I tell you the truth,' Jesus answered, 'this very night, before the rooster crows, you will disown me three times.'" Matthew 26:34

Pray It! Help me, God, to always take care of others.

Explore It! Why do you think Peter lied about knowing Jesus? Tell about a time when you took care of someone as Jesus asked His disciples to do.

God's Special Gift

What's missing?

Missing: tongues of fire

God's Special Gift

Acts 1:1–8, 2:1–39

After Jesus died, He stayed on earth for 40 days. One day, Jesus appeared to the disciples as they were eating.

Jesus told the disciples, "Do not leave Jerusalem. Wait for the gift that My Father has promised. John baptized with water, but you will be baptized with the Holy Spirit."

Jesus said that the disciples would receive a special gift. The Holy Spirit would come to them. He would give them power to preach anywhere in the world. After He said this, Jesus was taken up to the sky, and a cloud covered Him.

The disciples were together in a house in Jerusalem. A powerful sound came from heaven. It was like a strong wind filling the house. Flames appeared above the disciples. The flames were shaped like long ribbons or tongues. A tongue of fire touched each disciple.

The disciples were filled with the Holy Spirit. They began speaking in languages that they had never spoken before.

Many people heard the loud sound. They gathered around the house. The people asked, "How do these men know all of our languages?"

Peter told the people, "God has raised Jesus to life. He has given us the Holy Spirit that you now see and hear."

The people asked Peter what Jesus wanted them to do. Peter said, "First, you should be sorry for your sins. You should be baptized in the name of Jesus Christ. Then, you will receive the gift of the Holy Spirit. This is a promise to you and to everyone who comes to God."

Say It!   "'Therefore let all Israel be assured of this: God has made this Jesus, whom you crucified, both Lord and Christ.'" Acts 2:36

Pray it!   Thank you, God, that Jesus is with You in heaven.

Explore It! What were the disciples able to do after they were touched by the Holy Spirit? What promise does God give us if we come to Him?

Jesus Chooses Saul

What's missing?

Missing: beam of light

Jesus Chooses Saul

Acts 9:1–22

Saul put Christians in jail because they believed in Jesus. One day, Saul was walking to Damascus with his friends. They were looking for Christians to put in jail. On the way, a strange thing happened. A bright light from heaven flashed around Saul. He fell to the ground.

Saul heard a voice. It said, "Saul, why are you against Me?"

"Who are You, Lord?" asked Saul.

"I am Jesus, the one you are against," the voice answered. Jesus told Saul to go to the city and wait.

Saul's friends heard the voice, but they did not see anyone. Saul stood. He opened his eyes, but he could not see. Saul's friends led him to Damascus.

Saul was blind for three days. He did not eat or drink anything.

Jesus sent a disciple to help Saul. Jesus told the disciple, "Go to Saul. I have chosen him to preach My word to all people, even kings."

The disciple went to Saul. He said, "Saul, the light that you saw was the Lord Jesus. He has sent me to help you see again."

The disciple placed his hands on Saul. Instantly, Saul could see. Saul was filled with the Holy Spirit. He stood and was baptized.

Saul preached in Damascus. He told people that Jesus is the Son of God. They said, "Is this Saul? Is this the same man who took Christians to jail?" They were amazed by how Saul had changed.

Say It! "'. . . This man is my chosen instrument to carry my name before the Gentiles and their kings and before the people of Israel.'" Acts 9:15

Pray it! Father, thank You for forgiving even Your enemies.

Explore! It! For how many days was Saul blind? Name something that you have done to be a good person.

An Angel Frees Peter

What's missing?

Missing: broken chains

An Angel Frees Peter

Acts 12:1–17

King Herod did not like Christians. He ordered his soldiers to put Christians in prison. The soldiers killed some of the Christians.

James was one of Jesus' disciples. King Herod ordered his men to kill James. King Herod saw that this made the Jewish people happy. So, he put the disciple Peter in prison too. Four soldiers guarded Peter all of the time.

Christians knew that Peter was in prison. They prayed for God to help him.

Peter was asleep between two soldiers. He had chains around his wrists. Two guards stood by the door.

Suddenly, an angel appeared in a light. The angel woke Peter and said, "Quick! Get up!" Peter's chains broke and fell to the ground.

The angel said, "Put on your sandals. Put on your coat and follow me."

Peter thought that he was dreaming. The angel led him past the guards. The iron gate of the city opened by itself. Peter walked down the road. Then, the angel left Peter.

Peter went to a friend's house and knocked on the door. Many people were inside praying for him. A servant opened the door. She told the people, "Peter is at the door!"

The people were surprised and happy to see Peter. He told them how the Lord had sent an angel to free him from prison.

Say It! "'Now I know without a doubt that the Lord sent his angel and rescued me.'" Acts 12:11

Pray it! Father in Heaven, thank You for sending angels.

Explore It! Who gave the order to put Peter in prison? Who should you ask God to protect today?

Jesus Will Return

What's missing?

Missing: throne of God

Jesus Will Return

Revelation 1:1–2, 1:9–18, 21:1–27, 22:7–21

John was one of Jesus' disciples. After Jesus died, John taught God's Word. This made the king angry. When John grew older, he was put in prison.

One day, John heard a loud voice like a trumpet. The voice told John to write down everything that he saw.

John looked at who was speaking. It was a man with white hair and a long robe. He told John, "Do not be afraid. I am the Living One. I was dead, but now I am alive forever." John knew that the man was Jesus.

The Holy Spirit showed John a new heaven and a new earth. John heard a voice say, "God will live with people. God will wipe away their tears. There will be no pain or death."

John saw seven angels. One angel said, "You can believe my words. God has sent me to show you the future."

The angel showed John a city of gold and jewels coming from heaven. The main street of the city was gold.

A river flowed from the throne of God to the city. The water flowed into the middle of the street.

John heard a voice say, "I am coming soon! I will judge each person for what he has done. Some will come into the gates of the Holy City. Some will stay outside. I am Jesus. I am the Son of David."

John said, "Amen. Come, Lord Jesus!" John knew that Jesus would return.

Say It! "'He will wipe every tear from their eyes. There will be no more death or mourning or crying or pain, for the old order of things has passed away.'" Revelation 21:4

Pray It! We thank You, God, that someday we will live in heaven.

Explore It! Who did John see in his vision of heaven? What does Jesus want us to do to get ready for His return?